BOLD AS A LION

The Life of John Cennick
(1718-1755)
Moravian Evangelist

Peter Gentry and Paul Taylor

JOHN CENNICK

Dedication

**The Authors dedicate this book to their wives,
Frances Gentry and Margaret Taylor.**

Copyright © Paul Taylor and Peter Gentry

Published by Life Publications January 2007.

Book orders to – N. Seeds, 16 Linacres Road,
Leicester LE3 1RE

Tel. 0116 291 3045
e-mail ndseeds@yahoo.co.uk

Life Publications

Contents

Foreword   4

Preface   6

Acknowledgements   8

Abbreviations   10

Part One

1   A Berkshire Lad   13
2   Bristol Fashion   25
3   Chariots of Fire   37
4   Moravian Apostle   49

Maps and Pictures   68

Part Two

5   John Cennick's Theology   71
6   Evangelist and Preacher   93
7   Hymns and Poems   113
8   Cennick for Today   139

Appendices

1   John Cennick: Chronological Profile   152
2   Cennick's Personal Creed   155
3   Cennick's Published Sermons   157
4   Moravians and the Bible   160

Bibliography   162

Index   167

Foreword

Among the preachers and writers of the early days of the 18th Century Evangelical Revival in Britain John Cennick is one of the least known. This is partly because he has had little written about him. Yet he was important both as a 'Methodist' and later as a Moravian. His evangelical preaching was fruitful, he was highly esteemed by those who knew him and he was a hymn-writer of some importance. An unbiased and careful appraisal of Cennick's life and work is long overdue but now it has appeared. The authors, Peter Gentry and Paul Taylor, have done commendable research and have not relied on the information supplied by earlier writers on Cennick. Valuable facts have been gathered by visiting the places associated with Cennick's ministry, including Bristol and Dublin and also Gracehill and Ballinderry in Northern Ireland.

John Cennick comes alive in these pages and the authors are even-handed in their analysis of his strengths and weaknesses. We see him in conflict with John Wesley concerning the doctrines of predestination and Christian perfection. He leaves (or is dismissed) Wesley's 'Methodists' and joins himself to George Whitefield's followers. But after a few years he finds himself embroiled in the antinomian controversy that broke out among the Whitefieldites. In the authors' words, Cennick, 'in a weary desire to escape from theological argument...cast longing eyes at the Moravians and joins them in 1745.' For the next decade he travels and preaches and writes as an indefatigable Moravian itinerant and sadly dies at the early age of 36 in 1755.

Not only have the authors done their homework carefully but also they have given us a very readable account of Cennick's life. These pages are full of information about John Cennick but they are also a very enjoyable read. Dual authorship does not always, in fact seldom, result in stimulating reading that holds the attention but these authors have achieved that. The style is racy, conversational and engaging and these pages really hold our attention to the very end.

This new, well-written life of Cennick will interest Christians for a number of different reasons. It will certainly be of great interest to all who want to know more about the Moravians and the part they played in the 18th Century Revival. Likewise it will interest all those who want to know more about that Revival and especially this explanation of Methodist and Moravian attitudes to each other. It will be of no less interest to readers who want to widen their knowledge of Christian biography and this account of Cennick's life will not disappoint them.

Peter Gentry and Paul Taylor have done very fine research and writing and brought John Cennick to life. I warmly commend this very welcome book and I can promise it will not disappoint what I hope will be its many readers.

Dr Herbert B McGonigle
Nazarene Theological College
Manchester
July 2006

Preface

There is no modern biography of John Cennick although some writers have recently put us in their debt with work on his life and ministry. His name is surprisingly missing from some dictionaries and encyclopaedias of Church History where his valuable contribution to the 18th century evangelical revival would have merited mention. There are, however, articles in *The Blackwell Dictionary of English Biography 1730-1860*, ed. D M Lewis, 2 Vols. (Oxford, 1995) and also in *The Oxford Dictionary of National Biography*, ed. B Harrison, 60 Vols. (Oxford, 2004). Both articles are contributed by P J Lineham.

John Cennick's short life was marked with outstanding success and with a passion for preaching the gospel of Jesus Christ that merits an account of his work. The aim of the present authors is not to write an academic thesis but to make available a readable biography of Cennick's life and to examine some of the themes which captivated his mind and heart.

The format of the book perhaps needs a brief explanation. The first part, chapters 1-4, are biographical essays in which we have sought to present the salient features of Cennick's life in a form which, we hope, will encourage further reading. The second part, chapters 5-8, picks up various themes which have already been introduced and expands these into more detailed appraisals of important aspects of Cennick's thought.

A danger of dual authorship is repetition. We have tried to avoid this as far as possible. There are however events and features of Cennick's spiritual journey which are appropriate to his life and work and which also illustrate some aspect of the themes in the second part of the book. We hope that any overlap will not detract from the reader's enjoyment and the challenge of Cennick's life.

In his short life of 36 years Cennick had been influenced by his Quaker and Anglican heritage, his contacts with Whitefield, the Wesleys, Howell Harris, and latterly and more substantially by his association with the Moravians. All these influences, and others, eventually contributed to and cohered into the rather complex evangelical preacher of the gospel that John Cennick became.

Compared to John Wesley, Cennick's travelling was largely limited to London, Wiltshire, Wales and Ireland. Unlike Whitefield he was never drawn to America. Had he lived as long as his senior mentors and partners in the gospel, who knows where his preaching pathways might have led?

We are indebted to a whole panel of people who have helped us to compile this portrait of John Cennick and we have paid tribute to them in the next section. Without them our labours would have proved impossible and we offer our thanks to all of them.

Peter Gentry
Paul Taylor

Peter Gentry

Peter Gentry, a Londoner, was ordained in the Church of the Nazarene in 1961 and served seven pastorates in England and Scotland. He was editor of *The Flame* magazine from 1984 to 1996 and has written and published five small books. He has a Master of Divinity from Trinity Theological Seminary and a PhD from the European Theological Seminary. Now retired, he lives with his wife in Weston-super-Mare.

Paul Taylor

Paul Taylor was born in South Yorkshire. He is a Chartered Civil Engineer and worked for most of his professional life in Local Government. He has an MA in theology awarded by the University of Manchester after studies at the Nazarene Theological College, Didsbury. He is also Secretary of the Wesley Fellowship. Paul has two children and four grand-children and now lives in Leicestershire.

Acknowledgements

We wish to extend our thanks to the many people who have given their help as we have been writing about John Cennick. Some of them have played a significant role in the production of the book but all have been generous in giving their time and encouragement. Words of thanks are inadequate to express our gratitude. We simply say that without you the book could not have been written.

David Brace of Bristol has supplied useful information about Cennick's visits to the Bristol area. Margaret Connor's infectious enthusiasm for the Moravian cause and Cennick's connections with Fulneck have been an inspiration. The late Bishop J H Cooper and his wife Edna have put us in their debt, not only by Bishop Cooper's *Extracts from the Journals of John Cennick*, but in giving valuable information about Cennick's travels in the north of Ireland. We are greatly indebted to William T Graham who has generously supplied information from his wealth of historical and theological knowledge of the 18th Century. Dr Graham Greenlee of Belfast has provided information about place names in Ireland. We have greatly appreciated the help given by Peter Gubi, who has not only allowed access to his MA thesis *Whither John Cennick*, but has also introduced us to the treasures of East Tytherton. Thanks are due to Jonathan Hutton of Arnesby Baptist Church for the extensive use of copying facilities, often at inconvenient times. Beryl Johnston acted as a 'tour guide' as we visited some Cennick places in the Belfast area. We have had contact with John Little of Reeth who has been working on the life of Cennick for some time. We are also grateful for the encouragement of Dr Herbert McGonigle of Manchester who has spurred us on in his inimitable way and for providing valuable information. Much the same may be said of Jackie Morten and Lorraine Parsons at the Archive and Library of the Moravian offices at Muswell Hill. We acknowledge our particular indebtedness to the Moravian Church, Muswell Hill, London, who have readily agreed to our using documents from the archives. We should have been immeasurably poorer without the enthusiastic support of the Moravian Church House staff. We are particularly pleased that representative of the Moravian Church in London are of the opinion that the book is a balanced and fair account of Cennick's life and work. Mrs Ann Pursey, a Moravian, helped with background information of Cennick's work in Bath. Michael Rae allowed us to visit Ockbrook and uncovered the grave stone of Ann Cennick. Neil Seeds of Leicester has typed and retyped the script and has been inexhaustibly patient. Raymond Webb has provided information about the origins of the Moravian Church in Haverfordwest. We are also indebted to Anthony Lacey, an historian working at Leicester University for his helpful comments in the later stages of our work.

If we have inadvertently left out any friends who have helped we offer our apology and assure you that your contributions were appreciated.

We wish to express our very special thanks to our wives, Frances Gentry and Margaret Taylor, who for long months have been prepared to share us unstintingly with John Cennick. We appreciate their own distinctive brand of exhorting us to 'keep right on to the end of the road'.

Finally, we express our gratitude to Life Publications and to David and Jan Holdaway for their professional, expert and friendly assistance along the way.

Peter Gentry
Paul Taylor

Abbreviations

NIV	Scriptural references are based on the *New* International Version of the Holy Bible, Hodder and Stoughton (London, 1979)
CA	G Watson, ed. *Celestial Anthems: Poems by John Cennick,* Culver Press (Reading, 2001)
EJJC	J Cooper, ed. *Extracts from the Journals of John Cennick: Moravian Evangelist*, Moravian History Magazine (Antrim, 1996)
GWJ	*George Whitefield's Journals*, Banner of Truth Trust (London, 1960)
GWL	*George Whitefield's Letters,* Banner of Truth Trust (London, 1960)
JJW	N Curnock, ed. *The Journals of John Wesley*, Standard Edition, Epworth Press (London, 1931)
LHJC	J R Broome, ed. *Life and Hymns of John Cennick*, Gospel Standard Tract Publications (Harpenden, 1988)
LJW	J Telford, ed. *The Letters of John Wesley*, Standard Edition, Epworth Press (London, 1931)
MHB	*The Methodist Hymn Book*, The Methodist Publishing House (London, 1933)
MHBL	*The Moravian Hymn Book and Liturgy*, The Moravian Book Room (London, 1969)
NIDCC	J Douglas, ed. *The New International Dictionary of the Christian Church*, Paternoster Press (Exeter, 1974, 1978)
PWHS	*Proceeding of the Wesley Historical Society*, Vol. xxx, Pts. 2-5 (1955-1956)

SHCG   J Cennick, *Sacred Hymns for the Children of God in the Days of their Pilgrimage* (London, 1741)

SHRS   J Cennick, *Sacred Hymns for the use of Religious Societies* (London, 1745)

SOED   *The Shorter Oxford English Dictionary*, 2 Vols. (Oxford, 1983)

TMHS   *Transactions of the Moravian Historical Society*, Vol. xvi, Pt. 3 (1957)

WJWBE   F Hilderbrandt and O Beckerlegge, eds. *The Works of John Wesley*, Bicentennial Edition, Vol. 7, OUP (Oxford, 1983)

PART 1

Chapter 1

A Berkshire Lad
'An Episcopalian, every inch of me...'

A dark, a solitary way,
In search of him I trod;
And sick of love, and faint was I,
When lo! appeared my God!

(From a hymn entitled, *I slept, but my heart waked,*
G Watson, CA, p.50 and J Cennick, SHRS, Pt. 3, p.94.)

Reading is a nice enough little town, although few would claim much in the way of historical or architectural significance for it. Jerome K Jerome spoke of it as 'ugly Reading' but that was probably unfair. Historically, its associations are somewhat downbeat. King Henry I, who was described by Henry, Earl of Huntingdon, as 'in truth the most miserable' of English kings,[1] was buried there in the Benedictine abbey, long since reduced to ruins but still preserved. The unfortunate Archbishop Laud, one of the numerous victims of the duplicity of Charles I, was born in Reading, and Oscar Wilde wrote his *De Profundis* whilst a prisoner in its gaol in 1895-97.

In the annals of Christian history, Reading gained something of a reputation for spiritual unorthodoxy and was regarded as 'the town of many sects'. The Quaker historian, William C Braithwaite, writing of the visits there by George Fox and William Penn in 1653 said, 'The place had at this time the name of being a microcosm of all sorts of heretical opinions.'[2] Fox suffered there his 'hour of darkness and discouragement' in the home of Thomas and Ann Curtis.[3] A Quaker meeting was established there in 1655 and continues to this day.

This provides a fitting introduction to one of Reading's sons who shone brightly in the Evangelical Revival of the 18th century but whose contribution to it is generally underrated and, in these times, seldom even remembered. His name was John Cennick, and Dr A Skevington Wood's assessment that, 'No history of the eighteenth century awakening can be comprehensive which does not recognise the importance of John Cennick' is no exaggeration.[4]

Ancestry and Early Life

Cennick was born in Friar Street, Reading, on 12 December 1718 (New Style), the son of George and Anna Cennick.[5] His grandparents had been Quakers and suffered imprisonment there during the persecution endured by Friends in the reign of Charles II, but John's parents opted for the Church of England and devoutly followed its rites and responsibilities. These naturally included bringing up their four children strictly according to Anglican tradition, and John was duly baptised when three days old in St Lawrence's Church, Reading. This church still exists and is situated in Friar Street next to the municipal buildings (the old Town Hall).

The name Cennick is an unusual one and has given rise to a good deal of speculation as to its origin. There has even been some debate as to whether the initial 'C' is soft like an 'S' or hard as a 'K' would sound. An entry in John Wesley's diary where he refers to 'setting out with Sennick' would seem to settle the point.[6]

The Moravian historian, J E Hutton, advanced the idea that the Cennick family emanated from Bohemia, from which country, as Protestants, they fled during the Thirty Years' War in the 17th Century, and that the original family name was Kunik.[7] He cited no source or authority for this statement, however, and it has been carried over uncritically by later writers. Local Quaker records apparently refer to the grandparents by the name Connick or Cunnick, and some letters written by John Cennick, now preserved in the Moravian Church's archives, reveal that he had earlier signed himself 'Cunnick'. This would suggest that it was John himself who made the change to Cennick, but for what reason can only be conjectured. Graeme Watson, in a recently published study, researched the name extensively and considered that it could equally well have had a Celtic origin from either Wales or Cornwall.[8] It is perhaps significant that John Cennick himself, who wrote quite a long account of his early life and family roots, made no mention of the Bohemian connection and referred to his 'grandfather and grandmother Cennick'[9]. Further speculation is likely to prove unavailing.

John's childhood does not appear to have been a particularly happy one, and his adolescence even less so. He and his two sisters, Sally and Anna, were brought up very strictly, their mother apparently being the main religious influence upon them. John described the home regime as 'the worst of bondage and indeed cruelty', which does sound rather exaggerated but might well count as child abuse to modern minds! He referred to being kept 'strict to church' and forbidden any play on the Lord's Day but confined to 'read or say hymns all day long with my sisters'. If his father was indeed a schoolmaster as is conjectured, this would no doubt have made the home life even more rigorous. John envied other children who were not so restrained and confessed to rebellion, lying, anger and obstinacy.[10] All of this, of course, was written years later when reviewing his life before conversion and some allowance must be made for the tendency to over-stress sin so as to magnify the wonder of grace. Even so, the picture is an unhappy one and matters were probably made worse by the evident fact that John was a highly impressionable lad.

While still only very young, he was taken by his mother to visit her sister, who was very ill and near to death. He overheard his aunt witnessing to the maid who attended her to the effect that the Lord had stood by her bed in the night, invited her 'to drink of the fountain of life freely' and assured her that she should 'stand before the Lord bold as a lion.' These confident words of testimony affected him deeply, and when her joyful shouts of faith and joy caused his mother to exclaim with tears in her eyes, 'Poor soul', he was even more surprised when the dying woman instantly responded, 'Who dares call me poor? I am rich in Christ! I have got Christ! I am rich!' From that moment on, John prayed that he might have such an assurance of going to heaven. He spoke of these as 'the most early convictions I can remember.'[11]

They did not last, of course, and John's teenage years were marked by love of worldly amusements such as card-playing, horse racing and the playhouse, coupled with a fear of God and promising to be better. He longed for his independence and to be able to earn money for himself. When still only 13 years of age, he went to London, where an elder brother lived, in search of work and did actually begin a trial apprenticeship as a carpenter or possibly patten-maker. This came to nothing, however, as his master considered him too young to be taken on fully. Undaunted, he began to learn two or three trades in which he could work at home. By the age of 15, he had learned the art of buying and selling, and it seems that his mother actually provided a shop for him, but to no avail as he could not settle to anything. All this time, he was assiduous in church attendance and saying his prayers, chiefly, it would seem, to placate God, 'lest he should drop into hell before morning.'

The First Spiritual Crisis

The next milestone in John's painful journey to faith occurred in London and changed him from youthful levity to a state bordering on religious paranoia. He had again travelled to the capital in search of work and stated that while walking along Cheapside, 'the hand of the Lord touched me.' This put him in a state of fear and dejection in which he wrote, 'the terrors of the Lord came about me, and the pains of hell took hold on me.'[12] Gone now was the love of worldly amusements; instead, we see a nervy 17 year old who lived in a state of constant dread of judgment upon his sins, praying earnestly for pardon yet unable to assuage his feeling of guilt.

He took to hanging around the Abbey ruins in Reading, meditating upon his hopeless condition, even to walking all the way to Salisbury Plain, 40-45 miles away, and spending days, even nights, wandering around, eating only grass and nuts, in a vain attempt to escape the guilt that enveloped him. He exhibited all the signs of severe depression, petrified of the dark, seeing apparitions that taunted him and believing himself cut off from God despite his religious observances. He despaired of life and longed to die, yet was afraid of death.[13]

This went on for between two and three years, during which time, despite his psychological disturbance, he managed to find employment with a Reading man who put him to measuring land. Cennick has often been described as a land surveyor, but his work seems to have called for much less qualification that the title would suggest. Walking through fields where men were happily ploughing and sowing gave him a desire to join them but a fear of failure to manage horses and of being ridiculed prevented him. There were intermittent times when hope of salvation arose in John's mind, but always the sense of rejection returned. He toyed with the idea of entering a Roman Catholic monastery and even wondered if Jews or Quakers might have something better to offer, yet he writes, '[I] could not help mightily defending the faith of the church and of the Scriptures, though I stood in fear lest both should be but delusion.'[14]

Relief, however, was now near at hand for this tortured soul who felt himself to be reprobate. It was almost his despair and feeling that he had nothing to lose that took him at last to the place and time of deliverance. He had determined to make one final attempt to find peace by going away to a solitary place and resigning himself 'to the wise disposal of God.' Just what he meant by that is unclear. It sounds almost as though he did not expect to come back as he then paid all his debts in readiness for setting out in six days time, still hoping to find mercy but convinced that he deserved only hell.

Peace at Last

As he awakened on the day of intended departure, still full of foreboding and 'more dejected than ever', he heard the bells of St Lawrence's Church ring for prayers. Though at first inclined not to go, he did not wish to be thought negligent of his duties and since he would be gone by the same time the next day, resolved to obey the summons. The story of what happened in the church that morning is best told in Cennick's own words:

When I had entered the church, and fallen on my knees, I
began murmuring, as I often did, because my cross
seemed more heavy than ever was laid on any one beside;
and how untroubled all the children of God passed to
heaven, and how full of terror I must go down to hell!
And I was as if the sword of the Lord was dividing
asunder my joints and marrow, my soul and spirit; till near
the end of the Psalms, when these words were read,
"Great are the troubles of the righteous, but the Lord
delivereth him out of them all! And he that putteth his
trust in God shall not be destitute." I had just room to
think, who can be more destitute than I? when I was
overwhelmed with joy, and I believed there was mercy.
My heart danced for joy, and my dying soul revived! I
heard the voice of Jesus, saying, I am thy salvation. I no
more groaned under the weight of sin. The fears of hell
were taken away, and being sensible that Christ loved me,
and died for me, I rejoiced in God my Saviour. [15]

This landmark experience took place on 6 September 1737, three
months short of his 19th birthday.

Cennick's conversion bears all the hallmarks of that remarkable
chain of evangelical conversions among Anglican churchmen that
took place during the middle part of the 18th century and which
brought out the future leaders of the Evangelical Revival, beginning,
shall we say, with Howell Harris and George Whitefield in 1735 and
embracing such men as John Newton, William Grimshaw, William
Romaine, John Berridge and Charles Simeon. These were men
previously spiritually unlightened or of worldly disposition who, with
little or no contact with evangelical teaching, were gripped by intense
conviction of sin and after protracted seeking and wrestling with
God, experienced the new birth into the joy and peace of Christ and
the assurance of personal salvation. For the most part, they had little
or no contact with one another (until later, that is) or with anyone else
who would guide or counsel them. It was uniquely the work of the
Holy Spirit, the effects of which were profound and widespread.

Of the first year of Cennick's new Christian life we know very little, for the simple reason that he said little about it and was not yet in contact with any Christian group. He did record that very soon after his receiving the Saviour, he was sorely taunted by the Devil and tempted to doubt his salvation. After three days, however, during which his old mood-swings between hope and despair had returned, he experienced the peace of God in a way he had not known before and wrote, 'I believed the promise, and found the love of God again shed abroad in my heart; I saw clearly the will of the Lord in calling me through much tribulation, and I said gladly, "It is good for me that I have been in trouble."' The breakthrough came, he said, as the sun came out again after several dull days, reminding him, 'Thus shall the Sun of righteousness arise on thee.'[16]

It is, of course, quite common for early doubts to assail a newly-converted soul. The same thing happened in John Wesley's experience, and generally the nett result is good inasmuch as the new Christian learns to trust the Lord even more. It was so in Cennick's case; from then on, he says, 'he felt great and settled peace daily' and triumphed through prayer. A further problem for him was the lack of encouragement at home. He complained of 'the trials which I had from my own family...and the coldness which came from them.' We have already noted Mrs Cennick's lack of sympathy with evangelical testimony, so presumably her negative attitude persisted. John, however, declared that this only served to strengthen his detachment from the things of the world and his love for Christ.

Towards the end of 1738, someone, whose identity we do not know, lent Cennick a part of George Whitefield's *Journal*. This was published in seven parts, of which the first appeared in the spring of 1738 and was no doubt the one in question, as the remainder were issued over a period up to 1741. At first, he was unsure about reading it as he knew nothing of Whitefield and 'feared to read any books save the Bible and Hugo's Emblems',[17] but when he read 'the place where he mentions the woman who had been in the pangs of the new-birth,' he said, 'my heart cleaved to him, believing him not unacquainted with that bitter cup, the dregs of which I had long been drinking.' The passage referred to would appear to be Whitefield's entry for Saturday 14 January 1738, where he refers to being 'much pleased with the pious conversation of a poor woman, who was one of my auditors last night, and who, I believe, has passed through the pangs of the new birth.' He was then detained at Deal, in Kent, waiting for a favourable wind for his ship to set sail for America.[18] Immediately, John felt a great desire to meet the evangelist and began to pray earnestly for an opportunity to do so.

Not long after this, Cennick was invited to supper at the home of a local woman, where he met her son and a friend of his who was visiting from Trinity College, Oxford. When a game of cards was proposed, Cennick requested to be excused from taking part as he believed it to be a snare to faith and a waste of time. This prompted the visiting friend to exclaim rather sarcastically, 'There is just such a stupid religious fellow in Oxford; one Kinchin, whose brother is of our college and once as foolish as he, but is much otherwise now.'[19] Cennick rejoiced on hearing this for, as Hutton graphically put it, 'no longer did he feel like a pelican in the wilderness. There was somebody else in the world like himself.'[20]

With his usual quick determination, Cennick decided to go to Oxford and seek out this fellow Christian whose sense of unworldliness was so much like his own. Accordingly, on a wet Monday morning soon afterwards, he set out on foot for Oxford, a walk of some 28 miles, and upon arrival at the outskirts of the city, wind-blown and soaked to the skin, he realised the enormity of trying to find someone whose name he could not now remember, without any idea of his whereabouts. He was sorely tempted to turn back, but instead prayed, went on and found lodging for the night, uncomfortable though it was. Next morning, he enquired at Trinity College for the friend he had recently met and from him rediscovered Kinchin's name and that he belonged to Corpus Christi College. On the second day, he succeeded in meeting up with him and after conversation and prayer, was invited to join him for breakfast.

Although Cennick's expedition must have seemed rather like hunting for a needle in a haystack, the Rev Charles Kinchin would have been quite well known in the university. One of the members of John Wesley's Holy Club, he was a Fellow of his college and also held the rectory of Dummer, a Hampshire village near Basingstoke. In 1736, still only 25 years of age, he was elected Dean of his college and as this required his residence in Oxford, he was obliged to employ curates to attend to his parish. George Whitefield, James

Hervey and other Holy Club clergy frequently took turns of duty there. Thus did Cennick at length get to know Whitefield, whose *Journal* had first excited his interest, and before long he was in regular touch with Methodist fellowship. Kinchin himself died young in 1742.

Cennick's first meeting with Whitefield actually took place in London. Hearing from his new-found friends that the evangelist had returned from his first trip to America, he decided to lose no time and 'set out from Reading in the dusk of the evening and walked all night' to reach the capital. Contact was made at James Hutton's bookshop near Temple Bar and when they met, Cennick 'fell on his neck and kissed him.'[21] This led to an introduction to the Fetter Lane Society in which the Wesleys, Whitefield and Kinchin were involved besides a considerable number of Moravians. This was one of the Church of England Religious Societies of which there were then some hundreds, and it had become a focus for the new Methodist or evangelical revival movement then gaining momentum. In the spring of 1739, John Cennick, along with his sister Sally, whom he had earlier referred to as being 'very desirous of being born again'[22], and another Reading girl, Kesia Wilmot, a friend of them both, were received into membership of this group.

Meanwhile, back home in Reading, Cennick was making full proof of his Methodism by gathering a little Society around him. We learn of this from John Wesley's letter to George Whitefield dated 16 March 1739, in which he states that on his way from Oxford to Dummer to supply Kinchin's pulpit, he called in at Reading where, he says:

'I found a young man, Cennick by name, strong in the faith of our Lord Jesus. He had begun a Society there the week before; but the minister of the parish had well-nigh overturned it. Several of the members of it spent the evening with us, and it pleased God to strengthen and comfort them.'[23]

The visit is also recorded in Wesley's *Journal*, the diary date for it being 9 March 1739.[24] It was presumably the first meeting between John Cennick and John Wesley. From family correspondence, it is evident that Mrs Cennick no less than the vicar of St. Lawrence's frowned upon the little Society. Sally wrote that 'having preaching in the house...made a slur in the town and caused us much trouble and disgrace; so that my mother hearing of it in London, came home and put an entire stop to it.' [25]

Although Cennick, moving out of mainstream Anglicanism into Wesleyan Methodism, would become a Calvinist and finally settle as a Moravian, he never lost his love for the church of his baptism. When, much later in life, he was debating with a Presbyterian in the north of Ireland, he declared, 'I am an Episcopalian every inch of me and every drop of blood in me is Episcopalian.' He believed that Episcopal government was 'of divine authority.' [26] Cennick's conversion represents all that is best in Anglican spirituality, and in these present days of schismatic upsets in our national Church, it has a timely message that deserves to be heeded.

It was during his meeting with Whitefield in London that Cennick first heard of the evangelistic work going on in Bristol, particularly among the coal miners around Kingswood near that city, and Whitefield asked him whether he would be willing to become a master at the school which it was planned to build there for the miners' children. To this proposal he readily agreed, and Whitefield, it seems, offered there and then to write to Wesley on the subject.

Accordingly, on Whit Monday 11 June 1739, Cennick set out with a friend to walk from Reading to Bristol, arriving there two days later.

References for Chapter 1

[1] K O Morgan, ed. *The Oxford Illustrated History of Britain*, Guild Publishing (London, 1984), p.119

[2] W C Braithwaite, *The Beginning of Quakerism*, Macmillan (London, 1912), p.201

[3] *ibid.* p.273

[4] A Skevington Wood, *The Inextinguishable Blaze*, Paternoster (London, 1960), p.160

[5] J E Hutton, John Cennick - *A Sketch*, Moravian Publication Office (undated), p.5 footnote

[6] N Curnock, ed. *JJW*, Vol. 2, p.150

[7] J E Hutton, *op.cit.* p.5

[8] G Watson, *CA*, pp. 4, 34

[9] J Cennick, *Village Discourses*, Matthew Wilks (London, 1844, originally pub. 1803), p.iii

[10] *ibid.* pp.iii-ix

[11] *ibid.* pp.iii-ix

[12] *ibid.* pp.iii-ix

[13] *ibid.* pp.iii-ix

[14] *ibid.* pp.iii-ix

[15] *ibid.* pp.iii-ix

[16] *ibid.* p.xi

[17] *ibid.* p.xii

[18] *GWJ*, p.108

[19] J Cennick, *op.cit.* pp.xii-xiii

[20] J E Hutton, *op.cit.* p.12

[21] J Cennick, *op.cit.* p.xiv

[22] J Cennick, letter in Moravian Church Archives, London

[23] J Telford, ed. *LJW*, Vol. 1, pp. 282-283

[24] N Curnock, ed. *JJW*, Vol. 2, p.149

[25] G Watson, *op.cit.* p.14

[26] J E Hutton, *op.cit.* p.5

Chapter 2

Bristol Fashion
'Honest John Cennick'

Nor life, nor death, nor fire, nor sword,
Nor all the joys earth can afford,
Shall draw my heart from Christ, my Lord!
No worldly wealth, nor power above,
Nor height, nor depth, my faith shall move;
Nor part me from my Saviour's love!

(From a hymn entitled *Holy Confidence,*
J R Broome, LHJC, p.139 and J Cennick, SHCG, p.73.)

Before we follow John Cennick to Bristol to begin the next phase of his life and Christian service, it would be well to look at that city and in particular at the reasons for its importance in the emerging revival movement in 18th Century England.

The port of Bristol at that time was the second city after London in both commercial and cultural influence with a population of c.30,000. Its natural maritime focus was westward and consequently its ships traded extensively with America and the West Indies. That meant inevitably that it had a strong connection with the slave trade, and it is a sad reality that the otherwise fine tradition of its local traders, known as Merchant Venturers, owed its wealth and power principally to that appalling enterprise. That is now recognised with a high degree of shame, but was then regarded as an economic reality and commercial necessity.

It was George Whitefield who first proclaimed in Bristol the evangelistic message that was destined to change the nation's heart and, ultimately, banish slavery altogether. Whitefield was a Gloucester man, born there in 1714, who had family connections in Bristol, and as the two cities are only just over 30 miles apart, he naturally visited Bristol fairly frequently. It was on one such visit to his sister there that he was first spiritually awakened while attending a service in St. John's Church on the old city wall in Broad Street. Later, as an Oxford under-graduate, he came into contact with the Holy Club through meeting Charles Wesley. These 'Methodists' were then entirely absorbed in high-church ritualism and works of social charity and consequently were quite unable to help the young Whitefield in matters of personal salvation, about which he was by then deeply burdened and they were as yet totally ignorant.

Thus it was that, entirely on his own, George went through a long and painful time of heart searching, penitence and ascetic self-denial before finally coming to trust entirely in the Saviour's finished work of atonement enabling him to experience the new birth and assurance of eternal life. This happy event took place sometime in the year 1735, the year in which John and Charles Wesley left Oxford to accompany General Oglethorpe to the new American colony of Georgia.

After his ordination in Gloucester Cathedral in June 1736, Whitefield, at John Wesley's instigation, also offered himself for service in Georgia and was duly appointed. Whilst waiting for an embarkation date, he preached missionary sermons to crowded congregations in London, Bath and Bristol, where his youthfulness and remarkable eloquence made a deep impression and caused quite a stir. On returning from his first assignment in Georgia early in 1739, Whitefield sought to re-establish this ministry in Anglican churches, but now found that the popular acclaim of his earlier visits had changed to hostility and churches where previously he had been almost fêted were now closed to him. During his absence abroad, 'Methodism', then the general word for spiritual enthusiasm of any kind, had been gaining pace and the church authorities were becoming antagonistic to it.

Gospel Trophies at Kingswood

Being thus denied official pulpits, Whitefield, taking his cue from the Welsh revivalist Howell Harris whom he had lately met, decided to take to the open air to deliver his message, and in particular reached out to the Kingswood area just east of Bristol, a one-time royal forest where coal mining was now carried on. The miners there were notorious for their wild and lawless ways and few attempts had ever been made to reach out to them. Whitefield saw them as ready for the Gospel and his preaching had the most remarkable effect upon them. The sight of unchecked tears running in whitened rivulets down their coal-grimed faces as they listened to the story of the cross and the love of God is one of the all-time triumphs of the Gospel. Some hundreds of these needy people turned to Christ, and it was to care for them principally that Whitefield urged the spiritually renewed John Wesley to come down and take charge of the work, as he was due to return to America.

Before leaving, Whitefield proposed the building of a school at Kingswood for the children of the mining community, selected a site for its location and, on 2 April 1739, prayed over a dedicatory stone erected on the spot for divine blessing on this further enterprise. By coincidence, this took place on the very day that the newly arrived Wesley took his first stand in the open air, preaching in a Bristol brick-yard 'to about three thousand people'[1]. Had they both known it, the die was being cast in two directions on that memorable day! Wesley overcame his objection to field preaching, and Whitefield, as it turned out, marked out his independence from Wesley owing to his increasing leanings towards Calvinism as opposed to Wesley's Arminian views. They remained friends but worked now in separate channels.

The fact that Whitefield had provided the initial impetus for the school, for which the colliers themselves collected the sum of £20 towards the cost, was behind his invitation to John Cennick to take the post of master there. Cennick recorded, 'He wrote of the same to Mr Wesley and received a pressing letter for me to come to him.'[2] Wesley himself took over the school project, purchasing ground with the money collected plus some of his own, and financing its construction entirely. It was duly opened in the spring or summer of 1740, providing not only facilities for teaching the local children but also a meeting room for the Methodist society. This building should not be confused with a separate establishment on an adjoining site opened by Wesley in 1748 as a boarding school for the sons of his preachers and officially known as Kingswood School. This was re-located to Lansdown, Bath, in 1851 and still exists on a Methodist foundation.

We need to digress for a moment to look at the original school more closely insofar as it had a bearing on Cennick's status among the Kingswood Methodists because this unfortunately became a contentious issue. Whether Wesley actually concurred with Cennick's appointment by Whitefield is open to some question. His words, 'I do not commend you with regard to our brothers Seward and Cennick', in a letter to Whitefield on 20 March 1739 might suggest otherwise.[3] Cennick's time in Bristol was an unhappy one for other reasons as we shall see, and two years later, Wesley, who was by then in dispute with Whitefield over Calvinism, was upbraided by him for having turned Cennick out from his position. Wesley replied, 'What, from being school-master? You know he never was so at all. You know he now neither designs nor desires it.'[4]

Thomas Coke and Henry Moore, whose 'Life' of John Wesley appeared as early as 1792, defined Cennick's duties as appointed by Wesley as, 'to pray with and exhort the Society at Kingswood, as well as to superintend the school during his absence.'[5] The well-known biography of Selina, Countess of Huntingdon, which, although anonymous, is widely ascribed to A C H Seymour, is often regarded as a rather untrustworthy source, but has probably summed up the position correctly by stating, 'Mr Wesley had formerly appointed Mr Cennick to reside at Kingswood with a view to meet the Society as often as he could, in order to confirm them in the ways of God, either by reading to them, or by prayer, or by exhortation.'[6] That being the case, Hutton must be either wrong in saying that Wesley 'offered Cennick the post of head-master'[7], or else was expressing Cennick's belief that he had. Wesley himself reported that 'two persons are ready to teach so soon as the house is ready to receive them'[8], naming them as Ramsay and Snowde (who both, as it happens, turned out badly and were never so employed) and on balance, Cennick's role as 'helper', as Abel Stevens described him, is probably the right one.[9] In a modern school, he might be classified as a class-room assistant rather than a qualified teacher.

Cennick Commences Preaching

The chief point of interest in Cennick's arrival at Kingswood, however, lies not in his status regarding the school but in his unexpected introduction to lay preaching. When he arrived in Bristol on 13 June 1739, Wesley was on his way to London in answer to an urgent summons. After two days spent 'in waiting upon God', Cennick and his companion, who is named as Br Ferne, were invited to go out to Kingswood where some 400-500 people were waiting under a sycamore tree for the appointed leader, whom Hutton names as Sammy Nathen, to conduct an open-air service.[10] Probably because of his having lately come on Wesley's appointment, Cennick was asked to 'read a sermon or expound a chapter' as the expected speaker had failed to arrive. Despite his natural reluctance to do something he would have regarded as highly irregular he consented and opened with prayer. He records, 'Scarce had we ended prayer when the young man came who was to read' but instead of doing so 'he could not consent, but entreated me, if I was inclined, to expound.' So John took the plunge and spoke to good effect, 'in so much that many believed in that hour.'[11] It was a defining moment both for him and for the Methodist movement as it was the first time that a layman had actually preached to a congregation.

Further opportunities were given to him, on one of which his hearers numbered 'about four thousand', to whom he discoursed on the day of judgment from Mark ch.13. Surprisingly, when Wesley returned, he did not demur at these proceedings even when urged by some to put a stop to them, but, wrote Cennick, 'rather encouraged me, and often took sweet counsel together with me as friends.'[12]

Two years or so were to elapse until the next known instance of lay preaching in the societies, when Thomas Maxfield took the step at The Foundery in London, causing Wesley to resist him at first until, on the advice of his mother, Susanna Wesley, he relented and sanctioned the lay preaching, which became a vital part of the Methodist story. It may seem odd that Wesley should disapprove of Maxfield when he had encouraged Cennick in doing the same, but this may simply show how effective Cennick was in winning souls. There was one other lay preacher at that time, Joseph Humphreys, who had begun in 1738 but was then a Moravian and did not join Wesley until two years later, thus leaving to John Cennick, almost certainly, the distinction of being Methodism's first lay preacher.

We do not, unfortunately, have Wesley's 'take' on how he viewed Cennick and his role in the work at this time and whether the relationship between them was really as warm as Cennick claimed, but there is nothing to suggest any other view than Wesley's appreciation of his keen commitment and youthful enthusiasm. Cennick wrote of his preaching throughout 1740 not only in Kingswood 'constantly' but also in Bristol sometimes to supply Wesley's place, and in a number of South Gloucestershire villages including Kendalshire, Syston, Bridgeyate, Hambrook, Tockington, Elverton, Westerleigh and Hanham; also 'on the Causey' (or Causeway) between Langley Burrell and Chippenham in neighbouring Wiltshire.[13] This was a very large sphere of influence for one so inexperienced and gives Cennick grounds for recognition as one of the foremost leaders of the new movement.

Storm Clouds Gather

This happy prospect, however, was of short duration and by the end of that year, storm clouds were beginning to gather with signs that increasing trouble lay ahead. John Wesley noted in his *Journal* for 12 December 1740 that he set out from London to Kingswood, 'having received many unpleasing accounts concerning our little society at Kingswood.' His diary for that date indicates that Cennick and two others travelled with him.[14] It seems that John Cennick himself had been the centre of the controversy that had broken out. He had developed two strong dislikes, one of which was Wesley's doctrine of Christian Perfection. The other was the unrestrained physical manifestations, such as shouting, screaming and falling in a faint, that frequently occurred under Methodist preaching, and even at times under his own. It almost seems as if Cennick associated the two things together, as though the preaching of a strong call to perfection overwrought on simple minds and caused hysteria. Hutton perceptively remarked of the perfection teaching, 'As preached by Wesley himself, it was noble; as preached by his followers, it was absurd.'[15] If there is truth in that, perhaps Cennick saw only what he took to be the results of folly and had given voice to his criticisms in a rather public and personal manner. Furthermore, and perhaps most seriously of all, he strongly advocated the Calvinistic view of election and grace which he had taken in from Whitefield, and which clashed with Wesley's Arminianism. The battle lines were being drawn between salvation only for the already elect and salvation for all who will repent and believe the Gospel.

According to Cennick's *Journal*, he had the strongest support in Kingswood, but that, 'the Perfectionists all this while strove daily with Mr Wesley against me.'[16] They were calling for Cennick to be put out of the Society, and Wesley, while resisting this persuasion, did nevertheless forbid him to preach in the school any more. Wesley tried, said Cennick, 'to persuade me to renounce my principles which he said were the very opinions of the still Brethren and...preached to prove their tenets wrong.'[17] This is most revealing, for it shows that Cennick's objections reflected his support not only for Whitefield and Calvinism but also for the Moravians. The Fetter Lane Society in London, of which Cennick was a member, was at this period becoming heavily influenced by a type of Quietism introduced by the German pastor, Philip Mölther, which ruled out any active seeking for grace until faith had taken hold in a penitent's heart through silent waiting upon God. It was on account of this false teaching that the Wesleys and their followers had, that very year (1740), pulled out of the Fetter Lane meeting and set up their own distinctively Methodist base at the old Foundery in Moorfields. If Cennick too had been influenced by this 'stillness' idea, as even Charles Wesley himself had briefly, no wonder he looked aghast at the rowdy scenes in Kingswood!

It must not be thought that Cennick was opposed in any way to the teaching of holiness, and we heartily concur with Hutton's claim that, 'If ever a man was a lover of righteousness, it was honest John

Cennick. He longed for perfection as eagerly as John Wesley himself.'[18] Where he went wrong was in personalising the issue and preaching against the Wesleys in their own Societies, a move that many clearly did not feel was honest. As John Pollock rightly commented, 'Wesley's quarrel with Cennick lay with his behaviour rather than his beliefs.'[19]

Wesley stayed in Kingswood and Bristol for just over a month, during which time he sought to meet the objections raised by both sides in the dispute. He was surprised by Cennick's apparently cold attitude towards him, but patiently tried to persuade him to adopt a more conciliatory position, stressing that he had no problem with those holding Calvinist views remaining in the Society so long as they did not set out to promote them and thereby unsettle the work. Obviously referring to that time, Wesley wrote nearly ten years later to Dr Lavington, Bishop of Exeter:

> A few of us had a long conference together. Mr Cennick now told me plainly he could not agree with me, because I did not preach the truth, particularly with regard to election. He did so, but without any rancour. We had a long conference but not a fierce one.[20]

The Parting of the Ways

But it was all in vain. Returning to Kingswood in mid February, Wesley found the situation no better and accused Cennick of doing wrong in speaking against him behind his back. There was a stormy meeting at which Charles Wesley recorded, 'Ann Ayling (or Allen) and Ann Davis could not refrain from railing. John Cennick never offered to stop them.'[21] Since Cennick would not back down, Wesley felt that he had no recourse other than to exclude him from the Society. At another meeting a few days later, Wesley read out the decision of the Kingswood Society to terminate Cennick's membership and proposed that each person present should choose which party they would support. The meeting then divided. Twelve men and a like number of women withdrew with Cennick and followed him to a nearby house, where they formed themselves into what was, in effect, a Calvinistic Methodist Society – the first ever. The date was 6 March 1741.

Some attempt must be made to assess the relative parts played by Wesley and Cennick in this unfortunate rupture in what had been so successful an evangelistic enterprise. Many have excused Cennick on account of his youth (he was still only 22) and lack of theological training. He was obviously very impressionable, and so keen as probably liable to be impatient of correction. If he was weak, as Wesley later branded him, he was weak in judgment, failing to understand the strength of Wesley's leadership and thinking he could undermine it. When he realised this, he blustered and tried to justify his actions instead of quietly withdrawing. He did, after all, owe Wesley a duty to inform him of his contrary opinion, which he seems not to have done until the disagreement surfaced in disruption. The Kingswood School and Society were clearly influenced by George Whitefield as well as Wesley in a way that Bristol and London were not, and Cennick might have thought that, being responsible to both leaders since both had appointed him, he was in fact answerable to neither and consequently free to be his own man, especially as his preaching was so much used by God. If he does not altogether come out of this episode with flying colours, he does not come out entirely discredited either.

Does any criticism have to be levelled at Wesley in all this? Certainly, Schmidt concluded 'perhaps he acted hastily'[22], and on the face of it, Wesley's charge-sheet against Cennick – 'tale-bearing, back-biting, evil-speaking, dissembling, lying and slandering'[23] – does seem a bit draconian. It has to be remembered, however, that much was at stake, especially, as William Leary reminds us, 'it became still more serious when several members of the Bristol Society supported Cennick.'[24] Heavy-handed Wesley may have been, but unjustified in the action he took, almost certainly not.

It is pleasing to note that the break-up of this partnership between the Wesleys and Cennick does not appear to have left any lasting bitterness. Charles wrote to him a long letter beginning, 'My dearest brother John C., in much love and tenderness I speak'. Though the letter was an admonishing one, it concluded in kindly tones, commending Cennick, 'to Him who commanded us to forgive one another, even as God, for Christ's sake, hath forgiven us.'[25] John Wesley meantime continued to appreciate Cennick's hymns, helping him prepare his first collection, which he composed while residing at Kingswood for the press, and even having Cennick's well-known grace, 'Be present at our table, Lord', inscribed on his special Wedgwood teapot! Nearly five years later, when Cennick was leaving for Germany to visit the Moravian community there after deserting Whitefield's connexion to join them, Wesley recorded:

> I took my leave of poor J(ohn) C(ennick), just embarking for Germany. I admire the justice of God! He who would never long be advised by any who treated him as a reasonable creature, is at length fallen among those who will make him as passive a tool as ever moved upon wire.[26] (i.e. as a puppet).

A slightly waspish comment, perhaps, and not altogether an accurate prognosis, but good natured enough.

Cennick for his part does not seem to have harboured any sense of grievance against Wesley for what happened but moved easily into the Whitefield camp to continue what he had been doing so successfully for the past two years.

References for Chapter 2

[1] N Curnock, ed. *JJW*, Vol. 2, pp.171-172

[2] J Cooper, ed. *EJJC*, p.5

[3] J Telford, ed. *LJW*, Vol. 1, p.287

[4] *ibid*. p.356

[5] T Coke & H Moore, *The Life of the Rev John Wesley*, J Robins & Co. (London, 1822), p.224

[6] A C H Seymour, *The Life and Times of Selina, Countess of Huntingdon*, by a member of the houses of Shirley and Hastings, W E Painter (London, 1844), Vol. 1, p.32

[7] J E Hutton, *John Cennick: A Sketch*, Moravian Publishing Office (undated), p.14

[8] N Curnock, ed. *JJW*, Vol. 2, p.323

[9] Abel Stevens, *The Illustrated History of Methodism*, James Hagger (London, 1858), Vol. 1, p.120

[10] J E Hutton, *op.cit.* p.14

[11] J Cennick, *Village Discourses*, Matthew Wilks (London, 1844, originally pub. 1803), p.xiv, xv

[12] *ibid*. p.xv

[13] *ibid*. p.xv

[14] N Curnock, ed. *JJW*, Vol. 2, p.406

[15] J E Hutton, *op.cit.* p.17

[16] J Cooper, *op.cit.* p.7

[17] *ibid*. p.7

[18] J E Hutton, *op.cit.* p.47

[19] J Pollock, *John Wesley*, Hodder and Stoughton (London, 1989), p.141

[20] J Telford, ed. *LJW*, Vol. 3, p.314

[21] J E Hutton, *op.cit.* p.18

[22] M Schmidt, *John Wesley: A Theological Biography*, Epworth Press (London, 1973), Vol. 2, Pt. 1, p.53

[23] N Curnock, ed. *JJW*, Vol. 2, p.430

[24] W Leary, *PWHS*, Vol. xxx, Pt. 2, p.33

[25] N Curnock, ed. *JJW*, Vol. 2, p.434

[26] *ibid.* Vol. 3, p.228

Chapter 3

Chariots of Fire
'Whitefield's Trusty Lieutenant'

Help us, O Lord, to persevere,
And more than conquerors prove;
Assist us manfully to fight,
And triumph in thy love.

(From a hymn entitled *In Time of Persecution,*
J R Broome, LHJC, p.26 and J Cennick, SHCG, p.137)

The break with Wesley did not at first bring about any material change in Cennick's life and Christian service. He continued to reside in Kingswood and looked after the spiritual needs of the little society that gathered around him much as he had when they were all Wesleyans. They were, of course, still Methodists according to the current labelling, only they were Calvinistic instead of Arminian (i.e. Wesleyan). Whitefield's people did not develop a name-tag of their own and never became a separate denomination. Many ultimately became absorbed in the Countess of Huntingdon's Connexion, but the inception of that organisation was still some years away.

Cennick's original Society of twelve men and twelve women grew quite rapidly and before long he was reporting, 'that we were about one hundred and twenty'.[1] As Hutton nicely put it, 'he began with two dozen and soon had ten dozen'.[2] The house of one Stephen Tippett, 'a little way from the London Road', became the regular place of meeting, and, as Cennick recorded, 'we kept our lovefeasts in the fields and many blessings were vouchsafed to us, our Saviour was in the midst of our meetings continually'.[3]

When the doctrinal troubles were at their height, Cennick had written to Whitefield, who was then in America, to inform him of the unhappy situation and urge him to return to England as soon as he could. He wrote to him again on 17 January 1741 when it became clear that matters were coming to a head, and it was this letter, which was somehow 'leaked' to Wesley and produced by him in one of the tense meetings at Kingswood that turned Wesley's mind firmly against Cennick on the grounds of disloyalty to those with whom he was in fellowship. In this letter, Cennick pleaded with Whitefield to, 'Fly, dear brother. I am alone; I am in the midst of the plague. If God give thee leave, make haste.' The entire text of the letter is printed in the standard edition of Wesley's *Journal*.[4]

The Wiltshire Mission

While waiting for Whitefield's return, Cennick used those evangelistic energies that were so characteristic of him to enlarge the sphere of his usefulness, justifying what Thomas Jackson very fittingly said of him, 'though not distinguished by extraordinary power of understanding, [he] was possessed of useful talents'.[5] He had already made several preaching forays into north-west Wiltshire and now gave his attention to developing these early contacts into something more organised. A tailor in Castle Combe named William Orchard, who had heard Cennick preaching to many people in the Gloucestershire village of Sodbury (whether Old Sodbury or Chipping Sodbury is not known), invited him to Castle Combe and do the same, which he did on 16 July 1740.

This picture-postcard village, now so popular with tourists, was then a thriving centre of the local wool industry and a place of some consequence. Something like a mini-revival broke out there through Cennick's ministry and this brought together people from numerous other villages round about who desired him to visit them and to these he now devoted his further efforts. The following is a list of the places in this area which he recorded visiting to preach over the next couple of years, and in many of which he formed Societies on the typical Methodist plan. The modern place-name spellings have been substituted for the older ones found in Cennick's *Journals* where the identity is clear:

Brinkworth (in Hutton, 'Brinkwater' p.31)
Chippenham
Clack (Bradenstoke)
Corsham
Dauntsey
Foxham
Hullavington
Kellaways (referred to as 'Tetherton-Callaways')
Kington Langley ('Langley' in *Village Discourses*, p.xvii) and West Kington
Littleton Drew
Lyneham
Malmesbury
Rowde (near Devizes)
Seagry
Somerford (Great and Little Somerford)
Stratton (presumed to be Stratton St Margaret, near Swindon)
Sutton Benger
Swindon
Tytherton (East and West Tytherton, always rendered as 'Tetherton' in Cennick's writings)
Upton Cheyney (near Bath, actually in Somerset)

In addition, there was a place named as Avon which modern maps do not seem to show, unless it refers to Bradford-on-Avon, and another called 'Broadstock', which might stand for Bradenstoke.

Cennick named Foxham as 'the chief place' and under date 4 May 1742 he described how the Society there was organised:

I took Br Gotly to Foxham, now the chief place, and here at their own desire I formed them into a Society. I kept a meeting and explained the nature of a Society and asked each about the experience of the work of grace in their hearts, then wrote down many of their names. The Brn Gotly and Bryant were elected stewards to meet and care for them when there was no minister.[6]

At Brinkworth, where the number of converts steadily increased in spite of persecution, land was given to build a meeting house, the foundation of which was laid on 3 August 1741. The formal Society there was started on 1 July 1742; Bros Bryant and Gotly being appointed to look after it. It is interesting to note that this same village again became a thriving centre of evangelism when the Primitive Methodists established a large circuit there nearly a century later in their heroic drive into that part of England.

In the place Cennick always called 'Tetherton', now identified as East Tytherton, he purchased a house and parcel of ground which was offered to him for preaching as the private dwelling used at Foxham was too small to hold the Society's numbers. The purchase was completed on 9 November 1742, and the cornerstone of the new chapel built beside the house was laid on 24 May 1743. Cennick preached in the orchard to the crowds who attended the event, and the house from this time became his home and the headquarters for the Wiltshire work. Besides the two brethren named as stewards, and some others, he was joined and supported in this mission by his sister Anna.

Despite the rough handling they often received at the hands of the mob, to whom Cennick's youthfulness and lowly demeanour would mark him out as fair game, there was something quite impressive about the progress through the countryside of this eager band of evangelists, as this extract from a letter which Cennick wrote to Whitefield shows:

> I set out for Roud (Rowde), a place a little on this side of Devizes. About fourscore of the people of God went with me on horseback, beside those who went on foot. I found all the way I went the Lord had gone out before his children, and those words were uncommonly sweet to me, 'chariots of fire, and horses of fire' (2 Kings 2:11). I was sure these were round about us. Every town and village through which we passed was lined with inhabitants who beheld us, terrible as an army with banners.[7]

Cennick amply justified the sobriquet 'The Apostle of Wiltshire' which has often been given to him.

Cennick and the 'Tabernacles'

In describing all this very successful work in the West Country, we have run ahead of events a little and must return to 15 March 1741 when George Whitefield arrived back in London from America. He lost no time in sending an urgent summons to Cennick in Kingswood to come at once to meet him in the capital:

> Hasten hither, my brother, with all speed, and then we shall see what God intends to do for us and by us. It is a trying time now for the church. The Lord give us a due mixture of the Lamb and the Lion.[8]

Whitefield found to his dismay that his work in London had suffered a serious reverse during his absence abroad. Without his dominant personality and resounding oratory, the Moorfields crowds had drifted away, while all the time Wesley's work, centred on the Foundery nearby, had been making rapid strides, to some extent at the expense of Whitefield's following. Some criticism has been levelled at Wesley for taking undue advantage of the situation, but the fact is that other elements were at work, spreading scare stories about the predestinarian doctrine and denigrating Whitefield himself who was not without his financial troubles (chiefly concerning his orphanage project in Georgia) at the time. He had to endure the personal sorrow of being shunned and even vilified by people who had been converted under his ministry, and it must have been immensely heartening to him to welcome this eager young colleague who was so anxious to join him. He duly appointed Cennick as his lay assistant, along with two others; Joseph Humphreys, who had previously been with Wesley, and Robert Seagrave.

Whitefield still had influential friends in London and during 1741 they erected a large wooden structure in Moorfields to act as a centre for his ministry. Hardly a chapel but more like a huge shed in appearance, it nevertheless provided shelter from the elements for those who gathered to hear the preacher. Whitefield is said to have been a little unhappy at the appearance of deliberately setting up a rival to Wesley's Foundery and called it his 'Tabernacle' in the belief that it would be only a temporary feature and was, in that sense, redolent of the Biblical Tabernacle raised by Moses in the wilderness. The name, however, endured and most of the later chapels built by his Connexion were known by the name Whitefield's Tabernacle.

Whitefield's work in London made quite a rapid recovery and soon he was off on his travels around the country, including two very successful tours of Scotland. During these absences, he left Cennick in pastoral charge of the Tabernacle and the two kept in touch by regular correspondence. From New Kilpatrick in Scotland to Cennick in London, on 15 July 1742, Whitefield wrote:

> Of all my fellow labourers' letters, I think yours come the sweetest to my soul. You do not forget the rock from whence you was hewn, and therefore the Lord will honour you more and more.[9]

To Cennick, almost certainly, must be given credit for much of the revival of Calvinistic Methodism in London in the early 1740s, this, be it noted, in spite of Whitefield's previous objection to lay preaching. Like Wesley, no doubt, he had found it to be indispensable in carrying on so extensive a work.

In the meantime, Whitefield had not forgotten his cherished plan to build a school for the colliers at Kingswood. His Journal records at least six occasions after he left Kingswood when he took up collections for the school.[10] These may have been enough to complete the building, but as Wesley states that he paid for its construction himself, it is hard to say what became of such funds.[11] No doubt, misappropriation or even theft cannot be ruled out. In any case, Whitefield was wise enough to realise that he could not now lay claim to the building and accordingly he despatched Cennick back to Kingswood, charged with building a new school which would also serve as a meeting place for his own people. On 8 July 1741 he writes to him there, sending him, '£20 donated by Mrs C to begin the society room at Kingswood', which he believed she, 'will make up to fifty'.[12] He went on to urge Cennick to lay the foundation immediately but to avoid 'building too large or too handsome'.[13]

A site was chosen in what is now Park Road, Kingswood, about half a mile from Wesley's school and the land was purchased from a local collier. There was some attempt by another landowner to claim manorial rights over it but the issue was not pressed to litigation and the 'Tabernacle' was duly completed in 1742. It was replaced for worship purposes by a new Victorian chapel built on adjoining land in 1851 but continued to serve as a Sunday School until quite recent years. A plaque on the front wall carried the wording:

> This building was erected by George Whitefield, BA, and John Cennick, AD1741. It is Whitefield's first Tabernacle, the oldest existing memorial of his great share in the Eighteenth Century Revival.[14]

This inscription is not strictly accurate as the wooden structure at Moorfields was the very first although not succeeded by a substantial building until 1753. The Kingswood one was the first of Whitefield's Tabernacles to be constructed in a permanent form.

In Labours More Abundant

The years 1741-1744 saw Cennick very fully occupied as Whitefield's principal assistant. He was also appointed a trustee of the London Tabernacle and divided his time between London, Bristol and his Wiltshire network of Societies. He also made the acquaintance of the Welsh evangelist, Howell Harris, like himself, an unordained preacher, who had been active throughout the principality and who also visited Bristol, Gloucestershire and London. He wrote on meeting Cennick at Kingswood, 'I had a Heaven indeed with my dear Brother Cennick, finding him born again, sound in the faith, giving the glory to God, holding Election and Perseverance.'[15]

The two joined forces in Wiltshire and on 23 June 1741 they had a particularly fierce encounter with a well-organised mob at Swindon, which Cennick described in graphic detail:

> We found a large company assembled in the Grove with whom I sung and prayed, but was hindered from preaching by a great mob who made a noise and played in the midst of the people, and then with guns fired over our heads holding the muzzles so near our faces that we were both black as Tinkers with the powder. We were not

afraid, but opened our breasts and said we were ready to lay down our lives for our doctrine, and had nothing against it if their guns were levelled at our hearts. They then got the dust out of the highway and covered us all over and then played an engine on us which they filled out of the stinking ditches till we were just like men in the pillory. But as they played upon Br Harris I spoke to the congregation and when they turned their engine on me he preached...After we left the people dressed up two images, called one Cennick and the other Harris and then burnt them.[16]

The almost jaunty way in which they outwitted the ditch-water pumpers (until their pump broke down!) goes to show how good humour in the face of great provocation often won the day in many a tight corner in those days of exhilarating evangelism. It was heroism at its best, though these men would never have regarded it as such.

Howell Harris was also the link with Calvinistic Methodism in Wales, in which Whitefield and Cennick were to play a significant part. That movement, initially quite distinct from the one in England, stemmed from the ministry of Griffith Jones, Daniel Rowlands and William Williams of Pantycelyn, augmented by the lay exploits of Harris, whose friendly contacts with the Wesleys and Whitefield resulted in their visiting Wales. It was to Whitefield particularly, however, that these men looked for inspiration and leadership. Largely at Harris' instigation, a conference was called for January 1743 to meet at a house called Watford, just outside Caerphilly, the home of one Thomas Price, a supportive lay-man. This house still exists and can readily be seen. The oft-reproduced illustration of this group in session there shows four ministers (Whitefield, Powell, Williams and Rowlands) and three lay preachers (Cennick, Harris and Humphreys). Whitefield was appointed Moderator of the organisation then set up as the Calvinistic Methodist Association, to provide leadership and structure to the network of Societies throughout Wales that had come into being through the labours of these men. According to A D Belden, 'The headquarters of the new organisation was to be the Moorfields Tabernacle, London',[17] thus strengthening the ties with the English work.

Just over a year later, in April 1744, a similar conference assembled in Cennick's house at East Tytherton, again presided over by Whitefield, accompanied by Harris, Cennick, Humphreys and six other preachers and exhorters involved in the running of the Wiltshire Societies. Cennick noted in his Journal that it was 'at my special desire' that this 'first Association of our ministers and preachers was kept in Wiltshire.'[18] The set-up was generally similar to the Welsh one and its ministers were given responsibility for the care of the work in London, Bristol, Kingswood, Gloucester and Wiltshire. The overall superintendency in England devolved upon Whitefield, with Cennick, Harris, Humphreys, Adams and Jenkins designated as assistant superintendents. It was further resolved that all the English preachers, at the invitation of their Welsh brethren, attend the Welsh Association to meet at Trevecca, the house of Howell Harris, that summer.

Another initiative taken by Cennick at about this time was his proposal that a conference be held representing all three groups in the Revival movement, Calvinistic Methodist, Wesleyan Methodist and Moravian, with a view to finding common ground and thus facilitate co-operation and remove rivalry. Whitefield and the Wesleys heartily endorsed the plan, but unfortunately it foundered through an objection on the Moravian side. Hutton would appear to be in error in putting the blame on Whitefield, who, he said, 'refused to come'.[19] Whitefield's whole outlook consistently favoured unity whenever possible; but, of course, Hutton was a Moravian!

In September 1744, Cennick broke new ground by visiting Exeter, a place thus far only lightly touched by the revival. His ministry in the city, where he spent nearly a month, caused quite a sensation so that stiff opposition was stirred up, in spite of which Methodism began to establish itself there. Just prior to that development, in the August of 1744, Whitefield embarked on his third voyage to the American colonies, and it would be nearly four years before his return. At least he would have had the satisfaction of knowing that he was leaving behind a flourishing work, well organised across the country and left in the charge of capable men such as Cennick and Howell Harris who were fully in sympathy with his doctrines.

Unsettled Again

Nevertheless, there were some clouds gathering on the spiritual horizon; was Whitefield, one wonders, aware of them even as he sailed? The fact is that John Cennick was again becoming unsettled. There was a certain naivety about him which had probably left him ill-prepared for some difficulties which, in his total joy and release in working with Whitefield and Harris whom he so much admired, he had not anticipated. Unfortunately, the perfectionist controversy in the Arminian camp had its counterpart in the Calvinist one and that was antinomianism, namely the belief that a Christian, having been divinely predestined and elected to an eternal salvation which he could not forfeit, was thereby relieved of any responsibility to keep the moral law. This wild idea was as soundly repudiated by sensible Calvinists as by Arminians, but it caught on and threatened a major upset, especially in the London Tabernacle Society from which one group headed by William Cudworth soon seceded.

The situation called for firm and decisive leadership and for this Cennick was temperamentally unsuited. Courageous as he was in the face of hostile crowds, he found grappling with determined controversialists a very different matter and his gentle and peace-loving spirit wilted under the strain of it. In a weary desire to escape from theological argument, he cast longing looks at the Moravians, who seemed to him to be remarkably free from it, and by the end of 1745, he was one of them.

The Tabernacle fellowship was stunned by this sudden development since Cennick was a very popular preacher and much loved pastor and it lost about 400 members following his departure. Some historians would have us believe that he was a fickle young man who could not make up his own mind. John Wesley once referred to him as 'that weak man' but that is surely too severe a judgment. In his work with Wesley and later with Whitefield, he showed a steady commitment and considerable resourcefulness. A fairer view would be that expressed by A W Harrison, 'A changeable man Cennick may have been, but his sacrificial labours for the remainder of his short life reveal few signs of weakness.'[20] Rev Matthew Wilks, one of Whitefield's successors at the London

Tabernacles at Moorfields and Tottenham Court, in his preface to Cennick's *Village Discourses*, gave this generous opinion with regard to Cennick's resignation which, considering the perspective from which it was written, certainly commands respect:

> Whoever understands the nature of religious communions, knows that by passing out of one society into another, a man does not always reflect disparagement or censure upon his former connexions; he may be convinced that the other will, upon the whole, better suit his views and feelings as an individual.[21]

Perhaps it is fair to suggest that Cennick was too little experienced to take on the heavy responsibilities that devolved upon him, particularly in church administration and that at heart he was an evangelist pure and simple, never happier than when campaigning for the salvation of souls.

References for Chapter 3

1   J Cennick, *Village Discourses*, Matthew Wilks (London, 1844, originally pub. 1803), p.xvi

2   J E Hutton, *John Cennick: A Sketch*, Moravian Publishing Office (undated), p.23

3   J Cooper, ed. *EJJC*, p.8

4   N Curnock, ed. *JJW*, Vol. 2, p.428

5   T Jackson, *Life of The Rev Charles Wesley MA*, Wesleyan Conference Office (London, 1841), Vol. 1, p.248

6   J Cooper, *op.cit.* p.10

7   J Cennick, *op.cit.* p.xviii

8   W Leary, *PWHS*, Vol. xxx, Pt. 2, p.35

9   *GWL*, p.409

10   *GWJ*, pp.304, 312, 316, 325

11   J Telford, ed. *LJW*, Vol. 1, p.356

12   *GWL*, p.271

13   *ibid.*

14   A D Belden, *George Whitefield: The Awakener*, Rockcliff Publishing Corp. (London, 1930), p.197

15   J Leighton, *Howell Harris: the 18th Century Exhorter*, The Protestant Truth Society, (London, 1972), p.35

16   J Cooper, *op.cit.* pp.9 -10

17   A D Belden, *op.cit.* p.146

18   J Cooper, *op.cit.* p.11

19   J E Hutton, *op.cit.* p.32

20   A W Harrison, *The Evangelical Revival and Christian Reunion*, Epworth Press, (London, 1942), p.106

21   J Cennick, *op.cit.* p.xix

Chapter 4

Moravian Apostle
'Here I Stand'

Thy Ministers of flaming fire attend,
And sing me sweetly to my Journey's End.
Then let me hear, and bid my friends adieu,
Say to thine Honour, 'Thou art good and true!
I've overcome! I live for evermore!'

(An extract from *Nunc Dimittis,*
G Watson, CA, p.100 and F Baker, PWHS, Vol. xxx, 2, 1955, p.43.)

W hen the first representatives of the Moravian Church came to England in 1728, it was quite naturally taken to be a German Church, based in Saxony. Moravia was a German speaking area of Bohemia, now in the Czech Republic but then part of the Austro-Hungarian Empire. In point of fact, however, the Church's origins go back, even if somewhat indirectly, to England and specifically to John Wycliffe of Lutterworth in Leicestershire 'the Morning Star of the Reformation' as he is often called. Wycliffe preached a thorough going reform of the papal system with its priestcraft, purgatory and idolatrous practices, and a more Bible-centred faith. The Moravians were Protestants half a century before Luther's Reformation thanks to their adherence to Wycliffe's views.

Unitas Fratrum

In 1382, there was an alliance between the royal houses of England and Bohemia by the marriage of King Richard II and Princess Anna of Bohemia. This resulted in a cultural inter-change between the two countries and Wycliffe's teachings reached Prague, where they were eagerly taken up by John Hus, Rector of Prague University and preacher of the Bethlehem Chapel in that city. This position gave him a degree of independence from the ruling church and he used it to spread Wycliffe's anti-papal doctrines, condemning in particular the sale of Indulgences and other excesses of the Church of Rome. Official reaction was only to be expected and Hus, along with his friend and supporter Jerome (not to be confused with the 4th Century scholar and Bible translator) were arraigned as heretics and burned at the stake, Hus in 1415, Jerome a year later.

Despite this, the many followers of Hus were not cowed but exerted a considerable influence as reformers and Bohemian patriots against the Holy Roman Empire which then ruled the country. After various internal upsets, sadly including even armed conflict, those who remained loyal to Hussite principles formed a group called the Union of the Brethren, or Unitas Fratrum in Latin, at Kunwald in 1457. They continued to exercise widespread influence, first as a spiritual movement and then, from 1467, a national church with its own episcopal ministry. With the onset of the Counter-Reformation however, severe repression set in against them. Many fled to Prussia or Poland in 1548, while those who remained, although for a time strong and even powerful, were eventually overcome by Jesuit intrigue and finally crushed at the Battle of White Mountain in 1620. A fearful retribution of all Protestants in Bohemia, including the Brethren, ensued. The few survivors eked out a precarious, wandering existence as 'the Hidden Seed' under the care of Bishop John Amos Comenius (or Kominsky, to give him his Moravian name), the noted educational reformer, chiefly in Poland and Hungary, those in the former country adding to Brethren already there from the earlier banishment. But for Comenius, what became the Moravian Church would probably have become extinct.

It was from one of these exile Unity Brethren enclaves in German-speaking, though Catholic, Moravia that, in 1722, a party of ten people – men, women and even some children – under the leadership of a Pietist Lutheran preacher named Christian David, set out on a one-hundred mile trek across mountainous terrain to find asylum and a new home on Count Zinzendorf's estates in Saxony. He was already known to Christian David as a Pietist who was sympathetic to persecuted believers, and when he heard of their arrival on his lands, he warmly welcomed them. Other groups of religious refugees, including more who belonged to the Unity Brethren, followed until a village community some 300 strong had built up at a hilltop location near Berthelsdorf, which they named Herrnhut, the Lord's Watch. They worshipped in the local Lutheran church whose pastor, Johann Andreas Rothe, was entirely supportive towards them, and in August 1727 a mighty outpouring of the Holy Spirit came upon them, leading to a renewal of the ancient Unitas Fratrum as a church under the leadership of Count Zinzendorf as their chief bishop. The Count was strongly influenced by the writings of Bishop Comenius in taking this step. It also marked the start of a remarkable overseas missions work sixty years before the beginning of the modern missionary movement, which is generally reckoned from William Carey's call to India in 1792.

The slave plantations in the West Indies and North American colonies first engaged their endeavours, and as London provided a convenient stopover and a good place to obtain shipping access to the Atlantic, contingents of Moravian workers began to arrive in this country. Many of them found congenial fellowship in the Fetter Lane Society in London. The interaction between Peter Böhler and John Wesley, leading to the latter's evangelical conversion in 1738 is well known, and contacts with Wesley's friend Benjamin Ingham, a Yorkshireman, led to the establishment of a Moravian community at Pudsey, near Leeds, for which Ingham donated the land. They named it Fulneck after a town in Moravia where Comenius had once been the minister. A similar settlement at Ockbrook, near Derby, was opened in 1750 with others following. Moreover, the Fetter Lane Society had become definitely Moravian by 1742, giving them a significant role in the 18th Century Evangelical Revival.

It may well be asked what prompted Cennick to join the Moravians, about whom, by this time, both Whitefield and Wesley had begun to be uneasy. Clifford Towlson regarded it as, 'one of the mysteries of religious history that a man who was so obviously sincere should, though a Calvinist, ally himself with the Moravians, with their tendencies toward universalism'.[1] In saying this he was confusing universalism, which denies the Gospel altogether, with universal salvation, which makes salvation possible for all who respond to the gospel by trusting in Christ, not merely for those predestined to it. Could it perhaps have had something to do with his supposed Bohemian origins? As mentioned in Chapter 1, this suggestion is generally traced to Hutton's *A Sketch* but it actually goes further back than that. A footnote in the *Standard Edition of John Wesley's Journal* states, 'Recently a volume on John Cennick has been published by Rev J E Hutton, MA.'[2] This would relate to 1911, when the *Standard Edition* came out, so on that basis Hutton's book, itself undated, would have appeared a year or two before then. But back in 1844, the Countess of Huntingdon's biographer, Seymour, had referred to Cennick as, 'This good man, whose grandfather had been a Bohemian refugee',[3] so clearly Hutton was calling on a tradition that was already in circulation.

It is far more likely, however, that the Moravians appealed to him because of their uncomplicated faith. They stood apart from both the predestination rigours of high Calvinism and the perfectionist idealism of John Wesley, simply emphasising the love of Jesus, and especially his sufferings, without tendencies to legalism and theological strictures. His warm, affectionate, almost romantic nature seemed to bond with their uncritical views. A further point in their favour would no doubt have been the endorsement of the Moravians by the Church of England, which accorded their ancient Protestant church the status of full communion, enshrined in an Act of Parliament. Always an Anglican at heart, Cennick said on uniting with them, 'I have indeed left my mother's house since I have been born of our Saviour, but I now come back.'[4]

Apart from any he would have encountered in the Fetter Lane Society, the first Moravian he appears to have actually met was Johann Toeltschig, the leader of their mission to Georgia, who came to Kingswood in 1739 to see for himself the work among the colliers. Cennick was evidently not too enamoured with him! 'He often came where I preached,' he wrote, 'but because he saw that Mr Wesley was about to break off from the Brethren in London, and knew that I preached not directly the same, he would not speak much with me, only told me he loved me and wished I had more experience.'[5] Later, when acting as Whitefield's assistant in London, Cennick had opportunity to meet other leading Moravians and seems to have struck up a particularly warm friendship with Bishop Spangenberg (or 'Spangleberg' as he called him!) saying in a letter of May 1742, 'I love brother Spangleberg (sic) dearly; my heart is with his heart in the Lord Jesus.'[6] According to Belden, Cennick admired Moravian practice so much as to introduce their system of 'choirs' at the Moorfields Tabernacle.[7] Choirs were segregated groups of married couples, single men, single women, widows and children, each with their own separate seating and singing arrangements in church services and each with its own leader, forming a kind of sub-fellowship within the congregation.

As soon as his mind was made up on becoming a Moravian, Cennick wrote to Whitefield, who was in America at the time, to inform him of the move but had to wait nearly two years for a reply, Whitefield having been ill for a long time. When it came, true to the man himself, it was large-heartedly free from complaint or blame and written in the warmest expression of Christian affection and goodwill. 'I wish thee much success,' he wrote, 'and shall always pray that the work of the Lord may prosper in thy hands,' adding, 'I would only caution thee against taking anything for gospel upon the mere authority of man.'[8]

Cennick's first act on becoming a Moravian was to arrange a conference of the stewards of the West of England 'Tabernacle' societies, including those at Bath, Bristol and Kingswood besides the Wiltshire ones, in order to secure their transfer to Moravian control. Bearing in mind that he had organised most of these, not as a freelance, but as George Whitefield's official representative, his eagerness to take them with him may appear disingenuous, but they seem to have been very ready to follow him. On 18 December 1745, they 'unanimously signed an invitation to the Brethren to come among them, proposing to give up themselves wholly to their care, giving them authority to alter, change or do whatever they should see fit among them and the societies under their care.'[9] This must have reflected the depth of their attachment to him rather than any doctrinal conviction one way or the other. There was, however, some reaction at Kingswood, where a group of Whitefield loyalists claimed possession of the building and actually forced their way in. The Moravians eventually built their own chapel nearby in 1757.

Cennick Visits Germany

Early in January 1746, Cennick, accompanied by a Moravian, John Paul Weiss, left London and travelled by way of Harwich and Flushing to visit the Brethren's headquarters in Germany. This had been transferred from Herrnhut in Saxony to Marienborn Castle in the Wetterau region, some 30 miles from Frankfurt-on-Main, and since 1736 had become Count Zinzendorf's residence and the operational base of the movement following his banishment by the King of Saxony from his estates on account of suspicions as to his motives in becoming head of a religious denomination. In the near vicinity were the main settlement named Herrnhaag with its own church, a theological college at Lindheim, where Cennick received some instruction in Moravian doctrine, and Ronneburg Castle where Zinzendorf had a prayer chapel in which Peter Böhler was ordained in 1737 for the work in Georgia but which the Moravians later vacated.

There was much liturgical ceremony and musical celebration here to impress the young Englishman so lately departed from the plain ways of Methodism, especially in the Herrnhaag church which was richly decorated with murals and ceiling paintings depicting Biblical scenes. These were said to have been completed by one of the brethren 'in less than six months.'[10] The artistic quality therefore may not have been all that good, but it was enough to make Cennick feel quite overawed, although he was equally impressed by the devotional life and easy simplicity of the people. He was twice invited to preach in the church, and for one whose preaching up to then, when not in the open, had been conducted in barns, cottages, schools and, most recently, a huge wooden shed, this must have been quite an experience. His visit ended on 21 May 1746 when he returned home after a heart-warming, yet humbling, experience which caused him to confess, 'I have indeed been a keeper of other men's vineyards, but mine own I have not kept.'[11]

Cennick had hoped to be officially received into the Church and commissioned to go to Ireland for the Moravian cause, but they kept him waiting 18 months for membership and he recorded that the Count, 'permitted me to follow my convictions without immediately sending me, only he wished me to succeed.'[12] This sounds like a perfectly reasonable probationary arrangement, but there is no escaping Cennick's disappointment, although his resolve to join them did not waver. The Moravian way was always to proceed slowly and cautiously about the Lord's work, while his own was the exact opposite. He was eventually ordained Deacon in London by Peter Böhler and Leonard Dober in September 1749. There is no doubting the Count's admiration for Cennick; according to Hutton, he called him 'Paul revived'.[13]

One point of considerable interest that should be noted at this stage is the apparent lack of any lasting impact upon Cennick of the troubles that were afflicting the Moravians. This period became known as their 'Sifting Time' and involved an undue emphasis on the physical side of the sufferings of the Lord Jesus in a maudlin way as something to be sentimentalised rather than held sacred. They developed ways of expressing their love for the Lord that to some minds bordered on the erotic and trivialised the most profound matters of faith. Tyerman dismissed this as 'pestiferous lusciousness'[14] and it laid the Brethren open to ridicule if nothing worse. Hutton's comment is probably about right that, 'they were not immoral, they were only silly'.[15]

Unfortunately, reports of these excesses spread beyond Herrnhaag where they began and reached Britain, causing John Roche to publish a pamphlet on what he called *The Moravian Heresy* in which he accused them amongst other things of antinomianism. An altogether worthier writer, though one regarded by Hutton as 'an ignorant scribbler',[16] was Gilbert Tennent, a much respected Presbyterian minister who was involved in the New England revival in which Whitefield had been prominent. Tennent being of Irish birth, his opinions were known in Dublin when Cennick opened his ministry there and caused him some initial problems. Arnold Dallimore thus summarised Whitefield's strictures on the Moravians, 'He abhorred the unctuous terminology of their "blood and wounds" teachings and viewed their claim to being undenominational as merely a means of enticing people to leave other denominations and join theirs.'[17] Some traces of this extravagance can be found in Cennick's writings of this period, especially his hymns, but on the whole he does not seem to have been unduly impressed by this folly, which thankfully soon passed.

The same can be said of another aberration of the 'Sifting Time', namely the doctrine of 'stillness'. This was propounded by Philip Henry Mölther, a Moravian who became pastor of the Fetter Lane Society, and who taught that since salvation is due entirely to God's action, those seeking it must leave everything to Him alone and therefore should not attend meetings, read the Scriptures or even pray. They should wait passively until they receive the assurance of faith and only then participate in the outward means of grace. This ridiculous hotchpotch of Quietism, Quakerism and Mysticism infuriated John Wesley and precipitated his withdrawal from Fetter Lane in July 1740 with about 18 others to form a Methodist society based at the old Foundery in Moorfields. Fortunately again, wiser counsels prevailed and 'stillness' became a thing of the past, though not before many had been taken in by it. Thankfully Cennick was not one of them and he went forward into the next and final phase of his ministry as soundly evangelistic as ever.

Cennick's Mission to Ireland

He was first invited to visit Ireland in August 1744 when two visitors from Dublin attended a service at the London Tabernacle and were very impressed by his preaching. They indicated that there was support for such a venture in Ireland and urged it upon him. Against his better judgment, he admits, Cennick agreed to visit the following summer, but it was the end of September 1745 before he finally set out. He made for Parkgate, near Chester, to embark for the crossing, but no ship was available because of contrary winds. After a fortnight's wait and two false starts when the wind failed to change as expected, he decided that the will of God was against the plan and returned first to Wiltshire and then to London. At the same time he wrote to the Dublin friends explaining the circumstances and keeping open the prospect of coming at a later date.

Once his move to the Moravians and his visit to Germany had been accomplished, Cennick lost no time in fulfilling this intention and on the very next day after his return from the continent, on 27 May 1746, he once more rode north and embarked at Holyhead, arriving in Dublin on 3 June. He was warmly welcomed and began his ministry in a rented chapel used by a Baptist group in Skinner's Alley. This small society had been gathered by a converted soldier the year before. Two significant omens of future blessing for the Moravian cause in Ireland were revealed immediately. One was that Cennick formed a close friendship with the leader of the local Baptists, Benjamin La Trobe, a graduate of Glasgow University just beginning his ministry, who subsequently joined the Moravians and was the first of a family line of their ministers, including one bishop. The other was the strange but unmistakable fulfilment of a prophecy uttered by the previous pastor, a man of Unitarian views whose congregation had numbered only a handful of people, who had told them, 'When I am gone, a man of quite different principles from those I have taught, shall preach in this house and his hearers shall be so numerous, that neither the meeting house nor the burying ground shall be able to contain them.'[18]

As it had been in a rural English county, so also in Ireland's metropolis, Cennick's preaching caused an immediate stir and drew enormous crowds. Windows had to be removed from the chapel so that those who could not gain admittance could hear. Congregations reaching a thousand strong were recorded. Remarkably, many Roman Catholics supported the evangelist; one said that the Pope could not preach so well, and even a priest is understood to have written to Cennick saying, 'God has blessed you with great talents, I never saw the like; if you make any stay in this town, you will make as many conversions as St Francis Xavier among the wild pagans.'[19]

But this early adulation soon turned to violent opposition and there were some ugly scenes. Despite this Cennick soon had 500 or so adherents and there was good prospect for the future. Besides the hard opposition, there was also some Irish banter which gave rise to ridicule at Cennick's expense. In the course of a Christmas Day sermon, he had reportedly declared, 'I curse and blaspheme all the gods in heaven but the Babe that lay in the manger, that lay in Mary's lap, the Babe that lay in swaddling clouts.'[20] These were rather ill-judged words and led to his being publicly lampooned as 'Swaddling Jack', his followers as 'Swaddlers' and even their meeting place as 'the Swaddling House'! The Methodists also had this jibe hurled at them, causing John Wesley to observe rather tartly that the man who coined it, 'probably did not know the expression was in the Bible, a book he was not much acquainted with.'[21]

The next development saw the beginning of Moravian work by Cennick in the north of Ireland, although this first effort was ill-starred. A grocer in Ballymena by the name of Joseph Deane, who was in Dublin on business, invited Cennick to visit his town where the local Presbyterian minister was, in his view, preaching false doctrine. On 6 August 1746, Cennick, accompanied by two fellow workers, set out on their three-day journey. Their reception was somewhat frosty but some meetings were arranged in a large room, although the atmosphere was not improved by the collapse of the floor while Cennick was preaching on 'Christ as the only foundation'. Mercifully, no-one was hurt and the meeting continued outside. The obvious feeling that this was some kind of ill-omen made the local clergy even more edgy and they decided to call in the Lord of the Manor, Captain Robert Adair, alleging that Cennick was a Jacobite trying to stir up rebellion, this being so soon after Culloden and the end of Stuart hopes. Adair, in a drunken state, came riding into the town while Cennick was holding an open-air service, brandishing a whip with which he struck the preacher and pursued him with sword at the ready but Cennick's friends hid him in a house from which he was able to make his escape in safety. The Captain's son fortunately came on the scene and led his father away. Cennick and his friends left Ballymena the same night and rode to Antrim. 'All the way,' he wrote, 'I felt the smart and pain of the blows I had received on my head, but my heart was quite cheerful and easy.'[22] The blows were not taken in vain, however, for the day came when the Captain repented of his ways and asked to be admitted to the Brethren's Church.

Two years elapsed before the next attempt was made in the north, during which time Cennick continued his ministry in the Skinner's

Alley hall, assisted by La Trobe and some others. He made two visits to England to consult the Brethren leaders in London and a second to Herrnhaag in Germany. Meanwhile, officials of the Dublin congregation took out a lease on their hall and put in hand some necessary repairs. The owners' representative, Mr Samuel Edwards, however, seems to have had an unfavourable attitude towards them, possibly because of the negative press the Moravians had been getting, and sought to bring about their removal by greatly increasing the rent. At the same time, he offered the lease to a Methodist, Thomas Williams, a man of somewhat dubious standing with the Wesleyans, who was holding meetings in the city and looking for better premises, offering to pay double the existing rent. By the time Cennick returned, John Wesley had appeared on the scene and some correspondence, on perfectly friendly terms, ensued between them. The three-years' lease taken by Williams had been assigned to Wesley, who immediately offered to give it up in favour of Cennick if he were indemnified against any financial penalties relating to bonds and covenants incurred under an assigned lease. Cennick does appear to have stalled on this not unreasonable demand and as it appeared that the Moravians were not going to proceed any further in the matter, the Methodists took over the premises. One cannot escape the feeling that the landlords were playing the two groups off against each other so as to increase their profit as both Wesley and Cennick appear to have acted honourably throughout. Cennick's congregation met in various smaller locations around Dublin until moving to another meeting-house in Big Butter (or Booter) Lane in March 1748. Shortly before then, Johann Toeltschig, whom Cennick had met nine years earlier at Kingswood, came over to assist in the work and although their first meeting had been somewhat cool, they now formed a cordial partnership.

The second northern mission, again undertaken at the instigation of Joseph Deane of Ballymena, began in June 1748 following the settlement of the Dublin congregation in their new premises. Some opposition was again encountered, although less severe than before, and assistance was given by a local Quaker who allowed Cennick the use of his field in which to hold a meeting. The opponents, however, scandalously accused Cennick of misconduct, which they alleged had been seen by a man of low character who was prepared to swear to it.

Cennick was later summonsed to appear before the Justices at Shane's Castle to take the oaths of Allegiance and Abjuration in his defence, but he voiced his scruples against the swearing of oaths (an echo from his Quaker heritage, perhaps) while affirming his loyalty to the King. In the end, nothing more was heard of the accusation, but good came out of it. Fearing there might be further complaints against him, Cennick appealed to the Bishop of Down and Connor, Dr John Rider, who invited him to his home and agreed to accept a signed letter of loyalty given on grounds of conscience regarding oath-taking. The Bishop encouraged him with the words, 'Well, Mr Cennick, you will have fair play in all my Diocese' and is understood to have urged his clergy, 'preach what Cennick preaches'.[23]

The work in the north of Ireland now began to take off, for with Toeltschig and La Trobe able to take care of the Dublin church, Cennick was free to give his undivided time to itinerant evangelism. Over the next seven years, he is purported to have raised up as many as 220 societies, an amazing achievement. These were spread over the counties of Antrim, Down, Derry, Armagh, Tyrone, Cavan, Monaghan and Donegal. In December 1748, he moved with his wife and family into a house at Crebilly, Co. Antrim, which became his home for the remainder of his short life. In the autumn of 1750, the network of societies was organised into four divisions, and at the following places chapels were built:

Crebilly	1748 (converted barn)
Grogan	by 1750
Doagh	by 1750
Ballymena	1750
Gloonan	1750
Ballinderry	1751 (Cennick assisted in construction)
Derryscollop	1751
Drumargan	1751
Glenavy	1751 (converted house)
Lisnamara	1751
Crosshills	1754
Cootehill	1754
Kilwarlin	1755

In addition, a new church was built for the Dublin congregation in Bishop Street and dedicated on 3 April 1755. By this time, the reported Moravian membership in Ireland was 2000, which suggests that some of the societies must have been quite small and possibly did not last very long.

Another remarkable prophecy rather like the Dublin one previously mentioned, was fulfilled when Cennick came to Ballybollon on 21 August 1750 where he preached in a field, 'because no house could hold the multitude that came to the meeting'.[24] Here at Ballybollon Fort, in Charles II's reign, the Scots Covenanter, Alexander Peden, had uttered the words, 'O fort, I change ye in the Name of the Lord! Never let anyone preach here any more until a bonny wee lad shall come frae England and preach the pure Gospel of our Lord Jesus Christ.'[25] And here he was! Another echo from that turbulent century was a ruined church at Portmore, near Ballinderry, and a house there which had once been the home of Bishop Jeremy Taylor, whose book *Holy Living and Holy Dying* had a considerable influence on John Wesley. Cennick held a conference there in March 1751.

Some celebrities of Cennick's own time also come into the story. The Lord O'Neil, Ireland's premier peer, sent him a cordial invitation to visit him at Shane's Castle, and Lord Rawdon likewise invited him to 'preach at Moira as he wished to hear him' and 'treated him in the kindest manner'.[26] This latter nobleman, who later became Earl of Moira, married Lady Elizabeth Hastings, the elder daughter of the Countess of Huntingdon, thus strengthening his ties with the Evangelical Revival. Cennick also recorded several meetings with the Primate of all Ireland, who, 'encouraged him to preach in churches in the South and the West of Ireland.'[27] He is known to have visited Wexford in July 1752, but that may have been as far as he went in those directions.

The Last Years

From May to July 1752, Cennick made a tour through England, starting at Bath where he had earlier formed a society for Whitefield's connexion but now established a Moravian one. Taking in London, Bedford, Northampton, Nottingham and Ockbrook, Derbyshire, he arrived in Yorkshire and preached throughout the area where Benjamin Ingham had pioneered and formed his network of Societies, which had become Moravian in much the same way as his own Wiltshire ones. The following year saw him in Wales where he spent some time in and around Haverfordwest in Pembrokeshire. Brethren preachers had previously held services there and in 1751 a regular meeting was begun in a malt loft on the quayside. This group invited Cennick to visit them and his ministry was so blessed as to lead to Haverfordwest being established as a Moravian Church in 1763, their only church in the principality. A chapel was opened in the following year but sadly closed in 1956. Its site is now occupied by flats known as Moravian Court.[28]

On his way back to Ireland from London in 1749, Cennick had preached in Leominster, Herefordshire, at the request of a group of Christians meeting there. He made a second visit on his way back the next year and Leominster was subsequently organised as a fully-fledged church in 1759. Adding in those at Kingswood, Malmesbury, East Tytherton and Bath for which he was directly responsible, there are thus five churches in mainland Britain remaining as his legacy. In Northern Ireland, there are a further three; Ballinderry, Kilwarlin and Gracehill.

It might seem that on the face of it this is a very meagre heritage from such a far-flung and effective ministry as Cennick's certainly was. The explanation has to be found in the policy of the Moravian church not to strive for numerical growth as a denomination but to foster spiritual renewal among existing ones, especially the Lutheran Church in Germany, exactly as its Pietist forerunners had done, and the Church of England in this country. Their main emphasis was missions in whatever part of the world they might be led by the Holy Spirit to enter. Thus it was that they pursued a very laid-back attitude in advancing local societies, such as Cennick formed in abundance, to the status of an official congregation or local church. This inevitably led to a drift away of people who otherwise would have increased the number of churches. As Hutton so well put it, 'the other societies had to wait so long that finally they lost their patience and died of exhaustion and neglect.'[29]

Cennick's true legacy is to be seen not so much as simply what remains in tangible form but in the shining example he has left of selfless devotion to evangelism and his passion for the salvation of souls. In that respect, his contribution to the Evangelical Revival in 18th century Britain came nothing short of John Wesley's and George Whitefield's, and Arnold Dallimore does him no more than justice in his belief that it 'produced no more beautiful and holy life than that of John Cennick, and it is a sad loss to the Christian world that his career has been so flagrantly overlooked.'[30] His influence lives on also in the hymns of James Montgomery for, as Telford reminds us, 'it is said that a volume of Cennick's sermons was the means of James Montgomery's conversion.'[31] His father, John, who was raised at Gracehill and educated at Fulneck School, was a Moravian minister and had been a disciple of Cennick. There is still a Moravian Fellowship in Dublin, which meets periodically in the Lutheran Church in Adelaide Road and in 2005 for the first time this group has been included officially in the Moravian yearbook, *Daily Watchwords*. It is as though the spirit of Skinner's Alley lives on!

John Cennick died in London on 4 July 1755 at the age of 36. He had landed at Holyhead a week previously having the symptoms of a high fever already on him. Resisting the persuasion of friends to rest and recuperate before completing the journey, he pressed on, though it is amazing that he managed to sit astride his horse for the five days' journey up to the capital. Having arrived at Fetter Lane, obviously very ill, he was tenderly cared for but lingered only a couple of days. His health had never really seemed a serious problem and the likelihood is that he suffered burn-out due to overwork, possibly aggravated by financial pressure and some consequent depression. He was laid to rest in the Moravian cemetery in Chelsea, where a simple memorial stone may still be seen.

Family Matters

In the summer of 1747, John Cennick married Jane Bryant of Clack in Wiltshire. It must be presumed that this was the same Jane Bryant who is named among the signatories to the Tytherton Conference resolution inviting the Moravians to take over the West of England

Societies. A thorough search in the marriage records held in the Wiltshire Records Office which date back beyond the 17th century has failed to find any trace of Cennick's marriage. So it must evidently have taken place elsewhere, possibly in London or Bristol. Peter Lineham gives the date of 12th July 1747 but does not give the place of the marriage.[32] The question of marriage came up while Cennick was first in Germany, and in a letter to Count Zinzendorf he admitted to preferring a single state while being willing to consider marriage if the Brethren advised it.

Revealing light is given in John Wesley's account of a meeting he had with Mrs Cennick senior in London on 26 October 1750, when she asserted that her John only married under pressure from the Brethren and went on to complain, 'I had four children, but three of them are lost. They take no more notice of me than if I were dead.' Mrs Cennick was probably only referring to her then living children. Records show that there were four others; two who died in infancy and two other girls who died in their adolescent years.[33] At the same time, she spoke bitterly about being ordered by the Brethren to quit her rooms in the house at Tytherton. Wesley prefaced his account of this interview by stating, 'I think it my bounden duty to declare the heads of our conversation'[34] though for what reason so long after Cennick had severed his links with Methodism it is hard to see if not to discredit the Moravians. Cennick referred in a letter of 7 June 1747 to his plan to give his mother two rooms in his house at Kingswood, where his sister Anna and her husband were living, as 'the greatest and best means of easing my own mind about her and making her easy in as much as possible.'[35] John's final journey to England in 1755 was undertaken in order that he might visit his sick mother in London. Hutton adds the information that Mrs Cennick senior attended services at Fetter Lane.

John and Jane Cennick had three children, all girls. The first sadly died in infancy. The second, baptised Ann Grove Cennick, lived only to the age of 15 years and was buried at Ockbrook in 1767. The youngest girl, Hannah Elizabeth, born in 1754, married in 1784 a Dutch-born Moravian minister, John Swertner, who edited new editions of Cennick's hymns in 1789 and 1801. They had two daughters, the younger of whom, Louisa, lived until 1866. Swertner was not only a hymn-writer and translator but also an artist of some accomplishment. A picture by him of the Pool of London and Shipping on the Thames, dating from 1801, was presented by the Port of London Authority as a wedding gift to the then Princess Elizabeth in November 1947.

Ten years after John Cennick's death in 1755, his widow married Thomas Moore, a Moravian textile merchant of Beeston, Leeds, where they lived until her death in October 1774. Thomas died two years later. John's elder sister, Sarah, who had joined the Moravians with him, and conducted women's meetings in Ireland, eventually became a Deaconess and ministered to the sisters at various centres in Germany as well as in Bedford, Fulneck and Gomersal, where her death occurred in January 1770.

References for Chapter 4

1 C W Towlson, *Moravian and Methodist*, Epworth Press (London, 1957), p.106

2 N Curnock, ed. *JJW*, Vol. 2, p.407

3 A C H Seymour, *The Life and Times of Selina, Countess of Huntingdon,* by a member of the houses of Shirley and Hastings, W E Painter (London, 1844), Vol. 1, p.32

4 J E Hutton, *John Cennick: A Sketch,* Moravian Publishing Office (undated), p.33

5 J Cooper, ed. *EJJC*, p.7

6 J Cennick, *Village Discourses*, Matthew Wilks (London, 1844, originally pub. 1803), p.xix

7 A D Belden, *George Whitefield: The Awakener*, Rockcliff Publishing Corp. (London, 1930), p.163

8 J Telford, *The Methodist Hymn-Book Illustrated in History and Experience*, Epworth Press (London, 1934), p.75

9 J Cooper, *op.cit.* p.14

10 *ibid.* p.17

11 J Cennick, *Diary*, (1740-1751, Archive ref. AB.130

12 *ibid.* p.25

13 J E Hutton, *op.cit.* p.65

14 L Tyerman, *The Oxford Methodists*, Hodder and Stoughton (London, 1873), p.184

15 J E Hutton, *History of the Moravian Church*, (1909), p.278; cited, A Dallimore, *George Whitefield*, Banner of Truth Trust (Edinburgh, 1980), Vol. 2, p.328

16 J E Hutton, *John Cennick: A Sketch, op.cit.* p.45

17 A Dallimore, *George Whitefield*, Banner of Truth Trust (London, 1970), Vol. 1, p.215

18 J E Hutton, *John Cennick: A Sketch, op.cit.* p.43

19 A H Mumford, *Our Church's Story*, Whightman and Co. Ltd. (London, 1911), p.253

20 J Telford, *op.cit.* p.75

21 N Curnock, ed. *JJW*, Vol. 3, p.472

22 J Cooper, *op.cit.* p.29

23 J E Hutton, *John Cennick: A Sketch, op.cit.* p.57

24 J Cooper, *op.cit.* p.44

25 J E Hutton, *John Cennick: A Sketch, op.cit.* p.57

26 J Cooper, *op.cit.* pp.48, 50

27 *ibid.* p.52

28 R Webb, supplied details of Moravian cause in Haverfordwest

29 A H Mumford, *op.cit.* p.251

30 A Dallimore, *op.cit.* Vol. 1, p.305

31 J Telford, *op.cit.* p.86

32 P Lineham, *Oxford Dictionary of National Biography*, B Harrison, ed. (Oxford, 2004), *John Cennick*

33 J Little, *John Cennick: Conflict and Conciliation in the Evangelical Awakening*, Congregational Study Papers (1992), p.32

34 N Curnock, ed. *JJW*, Vol. 3, p.500

35 J Cooper, *op.cit.* p.31

MAPS & PICTURES

Picture Captions

1. John Cennick, as a young man
2. St Lawrence Church, Reading
3. Gracehill Chapel, Antrim
4. Skinner's Alley, Dublin, in Cennick's time
5. Moravian Settlement, Fulneck, Yorkshire
6. Church Notice Board, Kilwarlin
7. Moravian Church, Lower Ballinderry
8. Moravian Chapel, Ockbrook, Derbyshire
9. Moravian Church, Kilwarlin
10. Ann Cennick's grave at Ockbrook
11. The Fetter Lane Brick
12. Whitefield's Tabernacle, Kingswood, Bristol
13. Moravian Buildings, East Tytherton
14. Castle Combe, Wiltshire
15. Moravian Burial Ground, Chelsea, London

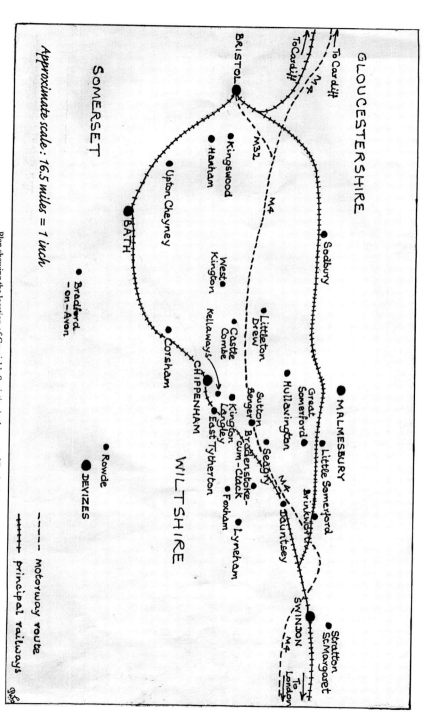

Plan showing the location of Cennick's Societies in the west of England

THE CHURCH.

1. John Cennick, as a young man

2. St Lawrence Church, Reading

3. Gracehill Chapel, Antrim

4. Skinner's Alley, Dublin, in Cennick's time

5. Moravian Settlement, Fulneck, Yorkshire

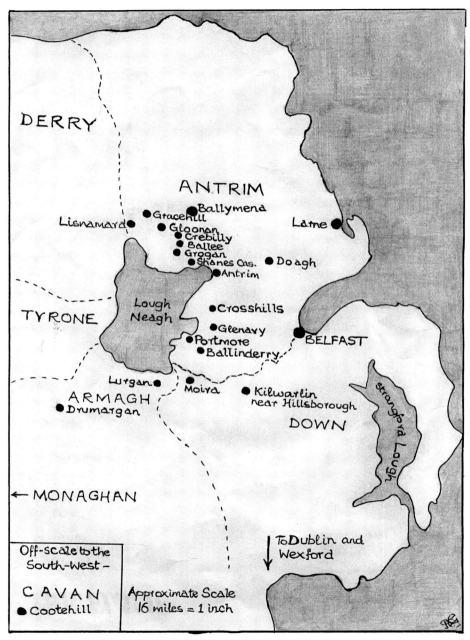

Plan of Cennick's Societies in Northern Ireland

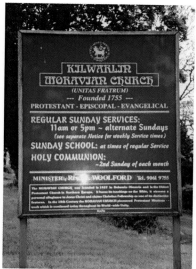

6. Church Notice Board, Kilwarlin

7. Moravian Church, Lower Ballinderry

8. Moravian Chapel, Ockbrook, Derbyshire

9. Moravian Church, Kilwarlin

10. Ann Cennick's grave at Ockbrook

12. Whitefield's Tabernacle, Kingswood, Bristol

11. The Fetter Lane Brick

13. Moravian Buildings, East Tytherton

14. Castle Combe, Wiltshire

15. Moravian Burial Ground, Chelsea, London

Picture Credits

1. From a block supplied by the Moravian Mission Agency

2. H E Greenside, Reading, from a sketch by H A Collins

3. Moravian History Magazine

4. Source unknown

5. From a sketch by John Freeman, 9 Market Place, Whitby, Yorkshire Y022 4DD

6. P Taylor

7. Beryl Johnson, Belfast

8. P Taylor

9. P Taylor

10. P Taylor

11. Sally Biggs, Bath

12. P Gentry

13. P Taylor

14. Photograph by Koji Sakai printed by the Sakai Litho Company

15. From a photograph by H M Knight and Judges of Hastings

Thanks are expressed to all the above sources for pictures used in the following pages.

The maps were drawn by P Gentry.

PART 2

Chapter 5

John Cennick's Theology
'Contending for the Faith'

God of the prophets(sic) power,
By whom the apostles spake;
Ride glorious on, send forth thy voice!
And let the nations shake.

With hearts and lips unfeigned,
We praise thee for thy Word;
We bless thee for the joyful news
Of our redeeming LORD.

(From a hymn entitled *After Sermon*,
J R Broome, LHJC, p.12 and J Cennick, SHCG, p.12.)

The development of John Cennick's theological understanding is a journey which takes in the influences of a Quaker background, Anglican upbringing, contacts with the Wesleys, his attraction to George Whitefield and his later settling more comfortably amongst the Moravians.

An assessment of Cennick's theology must take into account several separate but related factors. In the first place he did not enjoy the advantages of a classical education as did most of his famous contemporaries. Instead, during the intellectually formative years, Cennick was striving to settle himself into some sort of work and after his life-changing experience at the age of eighteen it seems he pursued his biblical studies largely unaided. Unlike the Wesley brothers he did not have the benefits of a spiritually sensitive and capable mother to supervise his secular and religious education. Rather, Cennick's youthful days were lived under the restrictive regime of an overbearing maternal supervision. So Leary can write, 'Cennick's mother exercised pharisaical principles in bringing up her children; regular attendance at the church and daily religious instruction'.[1] However well-intentioned Cennick's mother was, she did not produce in her son an enthusiasm for spiritual development as prevailed in the Epworth Rectory. It is much to Cennick's credit therefore, that he could stand side by side with John Wesley and George Whitefield and initially enjoy their approval. Towlson comments that John Cennick was a *'sui generis;'* the only example of its kind – unique; as much a master of his own craft as John Wesley was of his.[2] Indeed, Cennick's ideas were often developed independently of others.

John Wesley's well documented encouragement to his preachers to read widely and Cennick's early contacts with the Methodist preachers would provide him with ample recommendations for reading material. Wesley's *Christian Library* was produced to give advice on reading material to his preachers.[3] However, unlike Wesley's *Journal* references to books which had influenced him, those of Cennick contain little indication of his reading. Nevertheless if, as seems likely, his role at Kingswood included at least a modicum of basic tutorial work, those who were responsible for his appointment must have been satisfied that he had acquired sufficient learning to fulfil his responsibilities.[4]

Secondly, Cennick's theological journey involved serious disputes with Wesley's Arminianism and Whitefield's Calvinism and later, the confirmation of much of his doctrinal formulation by Moravian influence. He differed from John Wesley chiefly on the doctrines of free-will and Christian perfection. Cennick was also reluctant to endorse the emotional excesses which sometimes accompanied the preaching of the Wesleys, although they were not unknown as a result of Cennick's preaching. His diversion from Whitefield's Calvinism arose from the doctrines of rigid predestination and reprobation. There seems little doubt that one reason for Cennick's attraction to the Moravian Brethren was the more moderate tone of Moravian theology. The evangelical fervour and missionary zeal of the Moravians which he discovered to his delight on his first visit to Marienborn and Herrnhaag in 1746 cemented Cennick's mind and heart into the mould of the Brethren's theology and spirituality. Vulliamy, rather disparagingly and somewhat unfairly describes Cennick as 'a theological Proteus' (one who assumes various forms) and then comments that Cennick, during a controversy in which he found himself out of his depth, described himself, in an appeal to Whitefield, as 'a solitary Eli calling for help'.[5] Cennick's controversial ministry not only involved disputes and separation from the Methodists but in his later life he had to contend with the errors of Arianism (Unitarianism in one of its guises) and also those of Roman Catholicism. Against these, Cennick stood assured on a biblical platform. The body of doctrine with which he eventually became most comfortable was a synthesis of Anglican, Methodist and Moravian evangelicalism.

Again, Cennick was a notable figure in the 18th Century Awakening in Britain and his theological development was necessarily fashioned and nurtured in the furnace of astonishing activity. In the thirteen years from 1742 he travelled widely and often dangerously. Beginning in Bristol and Wiltshire, taking in part of Gloucestershire, he made his way to Ireland and Dublin, then to the north of the Emerald Isle and later into Wales and the north of England. He visited London on a number of occasions and Germany twice. In these 'journeyings often', he preached to multitudes, established societies, purchased lands, erected buildings, disputed with opponents, wrote carefully crafted sermons and journals and produced numerous hymns. In the midst of all of these many labours, he married and raised a family. Cennick's short life was one of constant labours for the Lord. He was not spared to live into the years of normal maturity, unlike most of his early contemporaries, and it is unwise to speculate as to whether his theology would have developed further in later years. The considerable number of societies and congregations which were established and churches built under his leadership however, pay eloquent tribute to the way 'the hand of the Lord' was upon him. In his own words Cennick expresses the purpose of his life and the focus of his ministry:

Arm'd with thy Spirit let me go,
And labour in the Field;
Contending earnest for the Faith
Once to the Saints reveal'd![6]

'The faith...once entrusted to the saints' (Jude 3) echoed in Cennick's verse, was the bedrock of his theology and armed as he was with the Spirit's power he contended for what he had come to believe and experience through life's varied journey.

The remainder of this chapter will seek to examine briefly three of the most important bench-marks of Cennick's theology; namely, his use of the Bible; his understanding of the Trinity and the pre-eminence of Jesus Christ; and his doctrines of sin and salvation. Other features of Cennick's theological make-up will be mentioned in the following chapters on his preaching and hymns.

The Bible

Cennick's chief doctrinal formulations were fashioned from his reading of the Bible as he possessed it in the *Authorised King James Version.* He read through the lenses of his own experiences, his differences with those who opposed him and the perceived needs of societies and hearers, as well as his familiarity with Anglican and Moravian liturgies. There is evidence that as early as 1737 he was applying himself to those Anglican expressions of doctrine, the Bible and the *Book of Common Prayer.*[7] From his early days at St Lawrence Church, Reading, he would be familiar with, if not enthusiastic for, the Apostles, Nicene and Athenasian creeds which were used in Anglican worship. Eventually those creeds did make their mark for he was to pen, in Dublin, his own confession of faith written in the form of a *Personal Creed,* in response to the defective Arian view of the person of Jesus Christ.[8] It will be necessary to return to this confession of faith with its affirmation of orthodox Christology later in this chapter. Meantime we return to Cennick's use of the Bible.

John Cennick's acceptance of the primacy of Scripture as the standard for believing and behaving is typical of the 18th Century evangelicalism as embraced by all the revival leaders. John Wesley wrote in 1746, echoing Luther's *Sola-Scriptura,* 'I want to know one thing, the way to heaven ...God himself has condescended to teach the way: ...He hath written it down in a book. O give me that book! ...Here is knowledge enough for me. Let me be *homo unius libri.*'[9] In Cennick's reverence for the Bible he was at one with the other leaders in the Awakening. For Cennick the Holy Scriptures are the words of God and are to be prized as an inestimable treasure.[10] If this is so, Cennick argued, his own response of faith must be to listen, to learn, to understand, to obey and to declare. A true minister of Christ believes the Word of Christ and teaches it.[11] He believed that God's Word, especially as it was heard in Jesus Christ, determined all doctrine, shaped the contours of personal faith and settled all controversies. Human reason, his own experiences and the traditions of the church are to be subject to the overriding authority of scripture. Those doctrines which clearly derive from the Bible, whether they please the world or not, are to be embraced, taught and lived. J Munsey Turner, in an essay entitled *Wesley's Pragmatic Theology,* refers to the quadrilateral of scripture, tradition, reason and experience, and argues that it is not an inaccurate summary of Wesleyan theological method.[12] Wesley 'did' theology in the way that was typical of Anglican theologians in the 17th and 18th Centuries, using what became known as 'the Anglican trilogy'; scripture, tradition and reason; going back to the Anglican Richard Hooker (1554-1600). Theology was constructed from scripture, aided by tradition and reason. As the 18th Century Revival progressed, Wesley came to make more of 'experience', carefully used, as an aid to how the Bible is to be understood.[13] Scripture was for the 18th Century Evangelicals, the 'centre of gravity' of their thinking; as George Croft Cell put it, 'Scripture is central, illuminated by the whole tradition, confirmed by the disciplined use of reason, verified in personal experience.'[14] In the use of the idea of a quadrilateral the longest side is always Scripture!

Cennick's approach to the Bible was refreshingly uncomplicated. The question of 'inspiration' which is to be found in various biblical texts (e.g. 2 Timothy 3:16) is assumed and affirmed rather than explained; he does not have any difficulty about the credibility or authenticity of biblical texts.[15] The literalism which this implies underpins Cennick's interpretation of scripture. His hermeneutical method is uncluttered by the biblical criticism which emerged in the next century and which resulted, whether intentionally or otherwise, in undermining the confidence in the validity and reliability of Scripture. Such a skeptical approach to scripture diminished the authority for matters of faith and practice which had prevailed since the Reformation. Cennick read the Scriptures starting from the assumption that the truths revealed may only be discovered through the work of the Holy Spirit illuminating what is otherwise dark. Although Cennick's favoured method of biblical understanding was a straight-forward literalism, this was often supplemented by the use of an allegorical form of exposition. An example of Cennick's allegorical, or extended metaphor method, may be seen in his treatment of the healing of Naaman (2 Kings 5) in which the whole discourse is based on the idea that leprosy is a 'figure' of sin:

> It [leprosy] was a disease that first broke out in a little white scab, and if not prevented or healed, overspread the whole body...How well doth the description serve to set out sin. It broke out first in Adam in one sin like a scab of the leprosy...it increased till he was altogether corrupt and infected...of him (Adam) we were all, and every one of us have from our birth this cursed disease.[16]

Cennick's understanding of the Bible was also strongly Christocentric. He would happily have found 'Christ in all the Scriptures'. V W Couillard writes:

> For Cennick, to receive Christ included assenting to the truth and validity of the scriptures and accepting Christ as He is offered and preached in the scriptures as our Lord and God, our only Saviour, our Righteousness, Wisdom, Holiness and Redemption.[17]

John Cennick's attitude to the Bible is perhaps nowhere more clearly expressed than in a recorded debate with Mr Arrat, a Scottish seceding minister and rigid Calvinist. The subject being debated was

Mr Dick

Thankyou for your
order.

→ book enclosed

Neil

reprobation and the event was conducted in front of about sixty people in the upper room of a public house in Moira (Co. Down, Northern Ireland). Arrat's final thrust was, 'It is impossible to hold to election and not reprobation'. Cennick's reply, which apparently ended the debate, illuminates his confidence in the Bible. He replied:

> I believe one and deny the other. I believe the Word of God, and what does not appear reconcilable with my judgment, I know, nevertheless, is possible with God, and clear as the light [to Him]. You, for the sake of the darling principle of reprobation, must either entirely leave out or wrest a good part of the Scriptures, whilst I, out of conscience, and a religious submission to God's Word, implicitly believe all.' For Cennick the matter was thus settled![18]

Cennick's understanding of the nature of Scripture and his use of it was an inheritance from his Anglican and Methodist days, but reinforced by the Moravian Brethren and echoed down two centuries from Martin Luther. In Arthur Skevington Wood's valuable work on *Luther's Principles of Biblical Interpretation* he writes:

> Luther's stress on the literal sense is related to his belief in the perspicuity of Scripture. He holds that the Word of God has "one simple, direct, indispensable meaning on which our faith may rest without wavering. The Holy Spirit is the plainest writer and speaker in heaven and earth and therefore His words cannot have more than one, and that the very simplest sense". So in his own exegesis he sets out to discover "the simple sense of His simple words".[19]

Cennick would have heartily endorsed the basic hermeneutic of the great reformer even if others more academic to follow would cloud Luther and Cennick's shining simplicity.

It has been suggested that Cennick's adherence to the Reformed view of scripture as the sole authority for faith and conduct was not shared in some Moravian circles. Notes on this apparent discrepancy are to be found in Appendix 4.

The Trinity and Jesus Christ

The 18th Century was a period when a radical form of Christianity rejected the orthodox biblical doctrine of the Trinity and the full deity of Jesus Christ. Unitarian heresy in the form of *Monarchianism* arose as a theological movement as early as the 2nd Century AD. *Sabellianism,* a development of Monarchianism, is named from its proponent, Sabellius, of whom little is known. He was probably an early 3rd Century theologian of Roman origin. The movement held a view that in the Godhead, the only differentiation was a mere succession of modes of operation. Thus, Jesus Christ was God only in the sense that a power or influence from God the Father rested upon his human person. *Socinianism* is so called after two Italian religious leaders, Lelio Sozzini (1525-1562) and his nephew Fausto Sozzini (1539-1604). Lelio Sozzini was at first associated with the Geneva reformers who later challenged his unorthodox Trinitarian views. His nephew Fausto was famed for the publication of a work on St John's Gospel in which he denied the essential deity of Christ. His anti-Trinitarian views were used to spread moderate Unitarianism in Poland. The Socinian teaching there was propagated through an academy at Racov of more than 1000 students publishing Socinian pamphlets throughout Europe.

In England, Unitarian doctrine came to prominence in the work of John Biddle (1615-1662) who published numerous Unitarian tracts to promote his anti-Trinitarian views. In the next century, Joseph Priestley (1737-1804), a native of Fairfax in Yorkshire and a scientist of repute, entered the Presbyterian ministry with Calvinist persuasions. (It was Priestley who had 'discovered' oxygen at his laboratory in Bowood House, Wiltshire in 1774). His theology became increasingly unorthodox and eventually he adopted Arian views of the person of Jesus Christ, also rejecting traditional views of the atonement and the inspiration of the Bible. His Unitarian doctrines were published in a popular work, *History of the Corruptions of Christianity* (1782). Four years later he produced his *magnum opus*, *History of Early Opinions Concerning Jesus Christ*, in which he defended his denial of the impeccability and infallibility of Jesus Christ. In 1791 Priestley became one of the founders of the

Unitarian Society. It was against this background of the Arian and Unitarian deviations that Cennick found himself, particularly in Ireland, defending his orthodox doctrines of the Trinity and his Biblical Christology. Arianism, against which Cennick issued his own *Personal Creed,* is usually regarded as a 4th Century Christological heresy, and was condemned as such at the first ecumenical Council of Nicea in 325AD. Arius (c250-c336) claimed to be a conservative Christian whose intention was to honour the monotheism of Apostolic Christianity. He did this however, by denying the deity of Jesus Christ as God's Son. At the same time Arius attempted to honour and worship Christ and even used the Trinitarian formula of Father, Son and Spirit. The high regard for Jesus Christ was the reason why Arianism had such a following up to the Council of Nicea and even expanded following the Nicene Creed. Arians afforded the Son the highest place next to God. Nevertheless, and notwithstanding that God is triune, God the Father and God the Son are utterly 'different in kind'. For Arianism, the subordination of the Son was essential to safeguard the unity of God. What alarmed traditional theologians such as Athanasius (296-373) was that the denigration of the Son detracted from the biblical doctrines of the incarnation and the atoning death of Christ. The use of the word *homoousis* in the declaration at Nicea to describe the consubstantiality between the Father and the Son was influenced by Athanasius in his disputes with Arius. The Athanasian insistence that the Son was 'very God' reflected Apostolic Christianity and corrected the crux of the Arian heresy.

The three important doctrinal formulations of the Anglicanism of Cennick's youth, the Apostles, Athanasian and Nicene Creeds all declared, for the assent of faith, the essential deity of each person of the Trinity. The *Apostles Creed* affirmed that Jesus Christ is God's only Son and sets the person of Christ in an historic context, 'I believe...in Jesus Christ, his only Son, our Lord, Who was conceived by the Holy Ghost, Born of the Virgin Mary, Suffered under Pontius Pilate, Was crucified...'. The *Athanasian Creed* is more explicit, 'And the Catholic Faith is this: That we worship one God in Trinity, and Trinity in Unity: Neither confounding the Persons; nor dividing the Substance. For there is one Person of the Father, another of the Son; and another of the Holy Ghost. But the Godhead of the Father, of the Son and of the Holy Ghost, is all one; the Glory equal, the Majesty co-eternal. Such as the Father is, such is the Son; and such is the Holy Ghost'. As would be expected, the *Nicene Creed* declares the deity of the Son in terms which reflect the Unitarian controversy surrounding its formulation, 'I believe...in the Lord Jesus Christ, the only begotten Son of God, Begotten by his Father before all worlds, God of God, Light of Light, Very God of Very God, Begotten, not made, Being of one substance with the Father.' All of this strong Apostolic and Trinitarian doctrine is enshrined in Article 1 of the Anglican 39 Articles which affirms:

> There is but one living and true God, everlasting, without body, parts or passions; of infinite power, wisdom and goodness; the Maker and Preserver of all, both visible and invisible. And in unity of this Godhead, there be three Persons, of one substance, power and eternity; the Father, the Son and the Holy Ghost.

This was the theological heritage of the 18th Century leaders who had been nurtured on orthodox Anglicanism. It was also the doctrinal foundation of Cennick's affirmation of Trinitarian orthodoxy from which he never wavered. In his *Personal Creed* he can affirm that, 'I believe that Jesus Christ...is verily, truly and eternally God' and 'I believe that God...made heaven and earth, and all the worlds, things visible and invisible; that he made me, body and soul...' As to the third person of the Trinity he can declare, 'I believe also and confess, (that)...His Holy Spirit has awakened and called me out of my sins, and made me to be concerned about my eternal state...'

V W Couillard, in a summary of Cennick's doctrines writes:

> The major emphases in John Cennick's theology are in God the Son, God the Holy Spirit and in the doctrine of salvation, with particular stress within the latter on the atonement and salvation by faith alone. Practically every sermon of his forty published sermons makes reference to these three doctrinal emphases. His Christological doctrine was completely developed and greatly stressed. His emphasis on the Holy Spirit is easily as great as that in

the Book of Acts. His doctrine of the atonement, of saving faith, and the utter inadequacy of other means of salvation is a persistent theme.[20]

Couillard is correct in saying that Cennick seemed to under-emphasise the Fatherhood of God. Only at the end of his *Personal Creed* does Cennick specifically use the term 'my Father'. He writes:

> I believe that a day shall come...(when) He (Christ) will confess me and not be ashamed of me,...To Him, with His Father, and my Father, and to the Holy Ghost, one Son, blessed for ever, be salvation and praise, henceforth world without end.[21]

J H Cooper, in his valuable *Extracts from the Journals of John Cennick*, comments on Cennick's work in the north of Ireland:

> Theological debates or disputes were common, especially relating to "Christ's Eternal Godhead". Cennick was an able debater and could make his point so clearly from Scripture that many were impressed who had been against him.[22]

Cennick may have had no more than a basic form of systematic theology, but his practical theology was strongly developed in his evangelistic preaching, as well as in his frequent disputes. For Cennick, evangelism was presenting Christ. Couillard rightly comments, 'Cennick placed paramount emphasis on Jesus Christ... the Jesus of history and the Christ of experience...None of the Christological heresies are to be found in him.'[23] The dual nature of Christ was fundamental to his doctrine of the person of Jesus. Cennick writes:

> ...who is Jesus that his coming into the world is of such importance? He is the eternal God! He is that Lord, that Creator, and Divine Being...and who out of his tender mercy...came from his throne and majesty, and was incarnate, a man, a servant; and whose painful life...and

shameful death, was endured by him with this sole and
pure view, to save sinners.[24]

It is hardly possible outside the pages of the New Testament to
find a more carefully crafted Christological statement and it
expressed perfectly Cennick's evangelistic focus.
The influence of the Moravian Brethren on John Cennick's
Christological vocabulary has been examined carefully by Peter Gubi
in his excellent unpublished MA Thesis *Whither John Cennick?*
(Bristol, 1998). At the time that Cennick visited Germany in 1746 he
was an impressionable young man who had still to develop a settled
theology. Gubi explores the Moravian influences on Cennick's
thought as expressed in his sermons and hymns. The continental
Moravians were enthusiastically embracing a vocabulary to describe
the Person of Christ and the atonement which at best was eccentric.
So extraordinary were the expressions in use by Zinzendorf's
followers that the saving work of Christ described in dynamic but
restrained language by New Testament writers became bizarre. Their
'Blood and Wounds' theology, as it became known, made its
impression on the youthful Cennick so that the unfortunate Moravian
atonement language began to appear albeit with some restraint in the
writings of Cennick, especially in his correspondence and hymns. J E
Hutton writes:

> As long as Zinzendorf used his own mental powers, he
> was able to make his "Blood and Wounds" theology a
> power for good, but as soon as he bade goodbye to his
> intellect, he made the doctrine a laughing-stock and a
> scandal...He composed a "Litany of the Wounds", and the
> Brethren could now talk and sing of nothing else; "We
> stick to the Blood and Wounds theology. We will preach
> nothing else but Jesus the Crucified. We will look for
> nothing else in the Bible but the Lamb and his Wounds,
> and again Wounds, and Blood and Blood." They began to
> 'worship' the side-wound. "We stick to the Lambkin and
> his little side-wound. It is useless to call this folly. We
> dote upon it. We are in love with it. We shall stay forever

in the little side-hole where we are so unspeakably blessed."[25]

C Podmore comments, 'As early as October 1741 we find him (Cennick) writing to friends in terms of the developing Moravian spirituality, "Fly to the Wounds of a crucified Saviour, and hide safely there".'[26] That Cennick was for a time influenced though not overwhelmed by the Herrnhaag atonement vocabulary is shown in a letter to James Hutton in 1747. He writes:

> I wait here in the Lamb's hand while he teaches me to be nothing, to be a poor sinner, and to thank him for his redemption...in my heart [I] am glad in the Saviour and love his wounds. I hear Br Böhler has visited Wiltshire, Bristol and Kingswood, for which I thank very heartily our Lamb.[27]

It will be necessary to return to this rather strange-sounding language when Cennick's sermons and hymns are considered in later chapters. For the present, it may be concluded that at least in relation to Cennick's atonement centred evangelism, his doctrine of the person of Christ was sometimes couched in unusual language. In defence of Cennick's use of the typically Moravian vocabulary, it is possible to find similar terminology in Whitefield's sermons and in some of Charles Wesley's hymns. It was in a general way typical of the fervour and flowery language of the 18th Century. It may also be said that in Cennick's doctrine of the Trinity, though he emphasised the co-equality and co-eternality of the persons of the Trinity, his evangelistic preaching for the saving of souls inevitably led to a bright light shining on the person of God's Son as the only Saviour from sin.

Sin and Salvation

Of all the elements of biblical doctrine which Cennick adopted, none were more basic to him as an evangelist than those of human sinfulness and the way of salvation. Again, following the Reformers and Evangelicals of his day, he derived his doctrine of the origin and universality of sin from Scripture. He writes:

> Our fall in Adam...has made regeneration absolutely necessary;...All the law and the Gospel agree, "that in Adam all died". All have sinned and come short of the glory of God.

> The words of the Psalmist he interpreted in a literal manner. 'I was born in sin and in sin did my mother conceive me' (Psalm 51:5). Again he writes, 'All are gone out of the way, there is none good, no not one' (Romans 3:10-12). 'These are some of the many scriptures which prove the general and universal fall and decay, which is the reason why we must be born again.'[28]

He maintains, 'In this woeful condition was...all souls, when God looked down...and saw how all flesh had corrupted their way before him.'[29] Cennick alludes with approval, to the reformed doctrine of total human inability, after the fall, to make any effective response to God; an approval which would surely have been endorsed by Wesley, Whitefield and the Moravian Brethren. His view of original sin and human depravity leads him to declare that, by nature, sinners are '...children of wrath, giddy and careless'.[30] Couillard writes:

> He [Cennick] proclaims man's nature as sinful and depraved because of the original fall. He sees the roots of religion not in man but through God's visitation with the gift of faith through the Holy Spirit. He is not...clear in following any settled view of election...he indicates belief in election to salvation, but strongly opposes the view of election to damnation. With his view of election there seems also to be universal salvation taught, that would be akin to the Arminian view of conditional election. The apparent contradiction is resolved for Cennick, it would seem, by the fact that since Christ's crucifixion there has been a provision for all mankind and the fact that God wills the salvation of all, but man may refuse the divine offer. If this seems inconsistent with his view of faith as a

gift, Cennick seems to teach that faith is a gift of God, which like salvation, can be refused or accepted...Free-will and responsibility seem to be taught also. Likewise in his ideas of security and perseverance of the saints, he seems to teach both the possibility of falling, and the faithfulness of Christ who will not permit believers to be plucked out of his hands.[31]

This lengthy summary of Cennick's doctrines of human sin and salvation calls for some comments. Firstly, the imprecision implied by the constant use of 'seem' or 'seems' indicates how difficult it is to tie Cennick down in the strait-jacket of a particular theological system. His chief concern was not to systematise theology, but to preach Christ as effectively as possible whilst at the same time disputing with those who denied what he saw to be a clearly defined biblical revelation of mankind's predicament and the divine solution. Secondly, if Couillard's summary is fair, it is difficult to see how Cennick could be in such strong dispute with Wesley's Arminianism. Certainly his views are not consistent with Calvinism's absolute predestination, limited atonement, irresistible grace and unconditional perseverance. As Dr Herbert McGonigle writes, 'It was when these points were argued in an absolute way, that is, as 'high' or hyper-Calvinism, that Wesley found himself most at variance with his Calvinistic opponents.'[32] Thirdly, the use of the term 'universal' or 'universal salvation' calls for comment. Cennick did not mean to imply that all mankind would inevitably be saved, but rather that the Gospel in its world embrace was to be offered to all mankind and that it was possible for all who believed to be saved by the exercise of the faith given by God. In a sermon entitled *The Sower* on Mark 4:9 he writes:

No man cometh to me except my Father draws him... but then He adds, when I am lifted up then I will draw all men after me, I can quicken whom I will; and accordingly we can see how He commands the same disciples whom He had before forbid to go to the Samaritans or Gentiles, now, to preach the Gospel to every creature, and promises,

I will stand by you, I will be with you to the end of the
world.[33]

With regard to Predestination, the idea of double-predestination
adopted by Whitefield, was not to Moravian liking. Zinzendorf warns
Whitefield that if he did not unequivocally disavow double-
predestination, 'that mystery of iniquity', the Moravians would have
to oppose him directly.[34] It is clear enough that, influenced by the
moderating Moravian views, Cennick, although leaning towards the
Calvinist position, did not generally adhere to 'high' Calvinistic
theology. The overall impression gained in reading Cennick is that in
his early and somewhat immature years he absorbed some elements
of 'high' Calvinism without thinking through the implications for his
own evangelism. Clearly he was drawn to Whitefield's warm
personality, spirituality and oratory, rather more than to the more
austere and authoritarian character of John Wesley. It is therefore
possible that Cennick's early Calvinism was a result of his close
association with Whitefield and adopted before he realised all that it
entailed.

The doctrines of the sovereignty of God and human responsibility
constitute a paradox; a statement seemingly contradictory, though
well-founded or essentially true. The paradox is well illustrated in
Don Carson's attempt at resolution. He states, 'God is absolutely
sovereign, but his sovereignty never functions in scripture to reduce
human responsibility; and, human beings are responsible
creatures...but human responsibility never functions in Scripture to
diminish God's sovereignty'.[35] For all Carson's valiant attempt at
resolution, the paradox remains. It is the ultimate Christian mystery.
Both elements of the paradox are known, equally, only by divine
revelation in Scripture. The same paradox and mystery occurs in the
nature of Scripture as at the same time, the result of the divine
sovereignty of self-disclosure and human responsibility in hearing
and writing what is disclosed. Even more so, the paradox and
mystery occur in the person of Jesus Christ who in his nature
combined fully and equally divine life and human experience. Was it,
in part, this paradox and mystery which prompted the Apostle Paul to
confess, 'Now we see but a poor reflection...Now I know in part; then
shall I know fully, even as I am known' (1 Corinthians 13:12)?

Whatever is said of John Cennick's early leanings towards a strong Calvinism and his later more moderate views, his doctrines of salvation from sin were built on the atoning work of Christ on the cross as an expression of God's sovereign saving grace and the exercise of grace-assisted faith as the response of the human heart to God's unique redemptive work in Jesus Christ. So Cennick could express his doctrines of the atonement in this way:

> When he [Jesus] appeared in the world, it was in the person of Adam, as one who undertook to set the whole ruined state of mankind to rights, and take upon himself the blame, curse and punishment of all, and redeem and save his people with justice and equity, and carry away whatever evil came in by the first man.[36]

In that brief summary Cennick expressed the fulcrum of his theology of salvation. It is by the sovereign act of the substitution of the Son to bear the penalty of human sin that mankind is brought to salvation. The Saviour's substitutionary death on behalf of sinful humanity deals radically with the old nature from Adam and restores mankind to God. Cennick declares, 'Christ has died and suffered in our stead. He has borne our curse...'[37] and again, 'He (Christ) is Almighty God, who has left all in Heaven...and came down...to redeem lost souls out of slavery and service of Satan...'[38] In a Moravian-style vocabulary Cennick writes, 'Jesus Christ's righteousness, his obedience to death, his suffering, and wounds, and blood, are the only things that make a sinner clean, or cause him to stand boldly in the judgment.'[39]

The prominent Reformed and evangelical doctrine of justification by faith alone is also a strong strand in Cennick's theology. Couillard comments, 'With Cennick, justification is not built on the untempered mortar of the sinner's own works but is the free justification founded on the grace and righteousness of Christ'.[40] Saving faith as experienced and taught amongst the Moravian Brethren and the 18th Century evangelicals is more than an intellectual assent to propositions or creeds, it is also an assurance of sins now forgiven. So Cennick can write:

But they believe more; and herein they differ from such as (only) profess the truth, or have a form of godliness... for they know our Saviour, they have peace with him, they have got absolution and pardon from him, they have his righteousness, they have his Spirit, they have the foretaste...of their everlasting inheritance.[41]

Saving faith is thus distinguished from formal believing and is accompanied by repentance and the new birth. 'If you would know what repentance is,...it is that which is learned at the foot of the cross ...there he [the sinner] sees what sin is, and that it could not be purged away but by the blood of God.'[42] All the evangelical preachers of the 18th Century Revival stressed the vitally important doctrine of the new birth that accompanied saving faith. 'Faith is not of ourselves, it is the gift of God; it is not natural, it is from above... For one thing to have saving faith is to be born of God.'[43]

It may be said, in summary and conclusion, that Cennick's doctrines of human sinfulness and the way of salvation embraced the heart of Apostolic Christianity, the crux of Reformation theology and the best of 18th Century Evangelicalism.

References for Chapter 5

[1] W Leary, *PWHS*, Vol. xxx, Pt. 2, p.30

[2] C W Towlson, *Moravian and Methodist*, Epworth Press (London, 1957), p.256

[3] W T Graham, *Pupils in the Gospel*, Wesley Papers, The Wesley Fellowship (Lutterworth, 2002), p.36

[4] A G Ives, *Kingswood School in Wesley's Day and Since,* Epworth Press (London, 1957), p.256

[5] C E Vulliamy, *John Wesley*, Geoffrey Bless (London, 1933), p.96

[6] J Cennick, *SHCG*, pp.24-25; also J R Broome, ed. *LHJC*, p.33

[7] J Cooper, ed. *EJJC*, p4

[8] V W Couillard, *The Theology of John Cennick*, TMHS (1957), Vol. xvi, Pt. 3, p111-113

[9] J Wesley, *The Works of John Wesley*, Bicentennial ed. Vol. 2, p.105

[10] V W Couillard, *op.cit.* pp.114-115, *J Cennick, Seventeen Discourses*, number 15, p.9

[11] *ibid.* p.114, J Cennick, *ibid.* p.7

[12] J Munsey Turner, *Wesley's Pragmatic Theology*, P R Meadows, ed. *Windows on Wesley, Wesleyan Theology in Today's World* (Oxford, 1997), p.12

[13] H B McGonigle, letter to Author, *J Wesley, The Witness of the Spirit, The Works of John Wesley*, Bicentennial ed. Vol. 1, pp.267-313

[14] J Munsey Turner, *op.cit.* p.13

[15] V W Couillard, *op.cit.* p.116

[16] J Cennick, *Naaman Cleansed* (London, 1793), p.8, sermon preached at Bristol, 1743, see Appendix 3, C5

[17] V W Couillard, *op.cit.* p.115, *J Cennick, Seventeen Discourses*, number 21, pp.5-6

[18] J E Hutton, *John Cennick: A Sketch*, Moravian Publishing Office (London, 1909), pp.62-64

[19] A Skevington Wood, *Luther's Principles of Interpretation*, Tyndale Press (London, 1960), p.26, see also reprint in P Taylor and H Mellor, *Travelling Man*, Cliff College and The Wesley Fellowship, Moorley's (Ilkeston, 1994), p.102

[20] V W Couillard, *op.cit.* p.111

[21] J Cennick, *Personal Creed*, cited V W Couillard, *ibid.* p.112, see Appendix 2

[22] J Cooper, *op.cit.* p.27

[23] V W Couillard, *op.cit.* p.119

[24] V W Couillard, *op.cit.* pp.121-122, J Cennick, *Seventeen Discourses,* number 22, pp.7-8

[25] P Gubi, *Whither John Cennick*, MA Dissertation (University of Bristol, 1998), p.27

[26] C Podmore, *The Moravian Church in England 1728-1760*, Clarendon Press (Oxford, 1998), p.89

[27] J Cennick, *Letter to James Hutton*, Moravian Church Archives (London), cited P Gubi, *op.cit.* p.31

[28] J Cennick, *The New Birth*, (London, 1799), pp.3-4, sermon preached at Malmesbury, 1741, see Appendix 3, C3

[29] J Cennick, *ibid.* p.4

[30] V W Couillard, *op.cit.* p.133, J Cennick, *Seventeen Discourses*, number 13, p.17

[31] V W Couillard, *op.cit.* p.130

[32] H B McGonigle, *Sufficient Saving Grace*, Paternoster (Carlisle, 2001), p.2

[33] J Cennick, *The Sower*, p.5, sermon preached at Co. Antrim, 1748, see Appendix 3, C16, cited V W Couillard, *op.cit.* p.136

[34] C Podmore, *op.cit.* p.58

[35] D Carson, *A Call to Spiritual Reformation*, Baker Books (Grand Rapids, 1992), p.142

[36] J Cennick, *Village Discourses*, p.180, cited V W Couillard, *op.cit.* p.142

[37] J Cennick, *ibid.* p.107, cited V W Couillard, *ibid.* p.143

[38] J Cennick, *Seventeen Discourses*, number 10, p.18, cited V W Couillard, *ibid.* p.143

[39] J Cennick, *Village Discourses*, pp.199-200, cited V W Couillard, *ibid.* p.144

[40] V W Couillard, *op.cit.* p.145

[41] J Cennick, *Village Discourses*, p.202, cited V W Couillard, *ibid.* p.145

[42] J Cennick, *ibid.* p.201, cited V W Couillard, *ibid.* p.147

[43] J Cennick, *ibid.* p.36, cited V W Couillard, *ibid.* p.146

JOHN CENNICK

Chapter 6

Evangelist and Preacher
'The Way to God'

Glory to God who gave the Word!
And bid the preachers cry;
Who caused his will to be proclaimed,
And brought salvation nigh.

(From a hymn entitled *Before Sermon,*
J R Broome, LHJC, p.10 and J Cennick, SHCG, p.11)

Above all else John Cennick became an outstanding evangelistic preacher whose passionate love for God drove him to endure severe hardships in his search for the lost. Podmore goes so far as to describe Cennick as '...the English Revival's most prominent lay evangelist'.[1] Once established in his high calling to be a preacher, nothing could divert him from what he believed to be his life's work. As previous chapters have shown, his doughty defence of the evangelical doctrines of salvation was accompanied by his untiring zeal for proclaiming Christ as the only Saviour from sin. This chapter is given over to viewing Cennick's call to preach; some experiences in his preaching ministry; tributes to his work and a brief overview of some of Cennick's selected sermons. In Cennick's own words:

> On the 14th day of June 1739, the burden of the Lord came upon me, and unto this day, the Lord, according to his word, hath been a mouth to me, and through his abundant love, he hath kept me from all doubts and murmurings...[2]

In such confidence, Cennick testifies to his calling as a preacher. As Dallimore writes, 'Truly Cennick had heard the call to preach and "the burden of the Lord" had come upon his heart...He preached almost every day, and often twice a day but with great power and blessing till his dying day.'[3]

The calling of John Cennick to preach the gospel did not at first find favour with his friends and colleagues. Whitefield, in particular, was not in favour of 'lay preaching' and Cennick was not at that time ordained. An entry in the *Journal* of Charles Wesley for 16 May 1739 states, 'At Fetter Lane a dispute arose about lay preaching. Many were...very zealous for it. Mr Whitefield and I declared against it.'[4]

When Whitefield heard that John Cennick had begun to preach and that another unordained man had done the same he wrote to John Wesley, 'Honoured Sir: I suspend my judgment of Brother Watkins' and Cennick's behaviour till I am better acquainted with the circumstances of their proceeding.' He then anticipates a possible objection that Howell Harris, the Welsh evangelist who was unordained, had been preaching with great success and with the approval of his ordained companions. Whitefield continues in his letter:

> I think there is a great difference between them [Watkins and Cennick] and Howell Harris. He has offered himself thrice for Holy Orders; him therefore and our friends at Cambridge I shall encourage; others I cannot countenance in acting in so public a manner. The consequences of beginning to teach too soon will be exceeding bad. Brother Ingham is of my opinion.[5]

It seems that Whitefield's objection to Cennick's public preaching was not only that he was unordained, but that he was too young and inexperienced. Whitefield was soon to have his reservations removed as Cennick demonstrated the validity of his call by an unusual ability to preach the gospel and draw sinners to Christ. Dallimore comments, 'Cennick became not only one of Whitefield's closest friends and, for some time, his chief assistant, but a preacher of such power as to stand, in that day of great preachers, in the rank of the first four or five.'[6] In his valuable work on Cennick, J E Hutton writes:

> He often addressed thousands in the open air with rain coming down in torrents...He preached in old barns, disused cloth mills, and in village cock-pits. He slept in the old ruined church at Portmore...He sat by the roadside, cold and lonely, munching his meagre lunch of bread and cheese. If money was plentiful, he used a horse; if not he would walk twenty miles to preach.[7]

In these ways, and in many others, John Cennick demonstrated the authenticity of his call to be a preacher of the gospel and confounded his earlier critics by his success. Not only was Cennick's preaching effective in reaching the crowds with the gospel, there is no doubt that he was also a popular preacher. In May 1748, Joseph Deane, a shopkeeper from Ballymena, called on Cennick in Dublin. Although Deane was apprehensive about inviting him to preach in the north because of the probability of opposition, nevertheless, there were many who desired to hear him. Indeed, opposition worked in Cennick's favour as the hostility of some seemed to make crowds more anxious to hear the English evangelist. Referring to Cennick's ministry in Dublin, Hutton writes:

> He preached on average twice a day. If the people of Wiltshire heard him with pleasure, the people of Dublin heard him with rapture. The majority of his hearers were Roman Catholics. The first Sunday the folk were turned away in hundreds. If Cennick would have had St Patrick's Cathedral, there would not have been room enough for his hungry hearers...The people who wanted to get a seat (in the hall in Skinner's Alley) had to come three hours before the time. The windows had to be removed. The people were packed all around the doors. On Sundays they even had to squat on the roofs of neighbouring houses; they perched on every window-sill and wall; and Cennick...had to climb through a window and creep on the heads of his people to the pulpit.[8]

We are indebted to Cennick himself for confirmation of the extraordinary success of his preaching. He records in his *Journal* for Sunday 3 July 1748, 'I believe at least 10,000 heard me at Ballee'.[9] The severity of the opposition did not quench his joyful spirit which was a feature of his preaching. He writes, 'I went preaching from village to village with great cheerfulness and blessing of God'.[10] Five days later he could write:

> I explained the parable of the Sower to a vast multitude, among which were some ministers of the Scotch Church and many Roman Catholics. I stood at the foot of Dunehigh hill and the people sat on the sides, and all around me, and heard me with many tears and the most desirable attention...[11]

Small societies or groups of converts rapidly grew into congregations. His journal entry for 14 November 1748 has this record, '...I went with Bro Turton to Crebilly where we began our first Society with six persons only, and what is remarkable is that before this day 12 months no less than 600 belonged to it.'[12] Cennick preached in Leominster in October 1749. The visit aroused great interest; the people were impressed by his preaching and winning personality. In a pamphlet, prepared by Margaret Davis for the Leominster Bicentenary Celebration, she writes, 'Speaking from the Society's room, he stood at an open window so that the crowds assembled in the courtyard could hear him.'[13] Welsh congregations took the irrepressible and happy evangelist to their hearts. In July 1750, Cennick records his preaching in the Welsh town of Rhosgoch, 'I preached here...to about 500 and I...was overjoyed to see how eager and well the Welsh hearts received the simple preaching of the Cross.'[14] Some distinctive Moravian vocabulary occurs occasionally in Cennick's *Journal*. Of his visit to Builth in July 1750 he records:

> We came early into the town and were welcomed enough. Two clergymen, two Justices of the Peace, a dissenting minister, five or six of the Welsh preachers and Exhorters of the Methodists with about 600 more, heard me preach in the new chapel here. It was a time never to be

forgotten. It was as if the Lamb had stood bodily amongst us. All wept, and were sweetly affected.[15]

Occasionally Cennick and his brethren witnessed quite extraordinary scenes as a result of preaching which focused on what the Moravians called 'the Lamb texts' and on the blood and wounds of the Saviour. Here is his (abbreviated) hand-written account of such an unusual event:

> I had been appointed...to preach at Stratton...not more than three miles from Swindon at which time, as it was supposed, because I preached much about the Blood of Christ, the chief persons in the former mob got a butcher to save all the blood he could, that, as they said they might play it out...upon us, and so give us blood enough. But before I came to Stratton, God struck them with particular judgements. All the authors of this design, John and Thomas Violet, the Parson of Stratton, and Sylvester Keen, a bailiff, all bled at the nose and some at the mouth without ceasing, till one of the former fell into a dead fit, and could no more be trusted alone; the minister did not recover, for it brought him to his grave and Sylvester Keen continued to bleed at times...and on March 31st following he died, cursing terribly.[16]

This remarkable account illustrates that the opposition to gospel preaching occasionally produced unexpected results which were understood as the hand of God, both in blessing on the preaching and judgment on the scoffers. Pointing sinners in the way to God through the redemptive sacrifice of the Saviour was the heartbeat of Cennick's preaching. In a testimonial hymn he writes:

> *I'll tell to all poor Sinners round,*
> *What a dear Saviour I have found;*
> *I'll point to thy redeeming Blood,*
> *And say, Behold the Way to God!*[17]

Many tributes were paid to Cennick by his contemporaries and by those who have commented on the man and his preaching. Cennick's gentle and retiring disposition would never have sought the accolades of men; his chief concern during all of his active and energetic life was to please the Lord who had called him to preach the riches of the Gospel of redeeming grace in Jesus Christ. No man would usurp the place of Christ in his heart. Nevertheless, tributes paid to him are worthy of record.

Writing of Wesley's choice of Cennick for the work, Luke Tyerman, in *John Wesley, His Life and Times* writes:

> In no man was there a greater combination of docility and courage; and hence, when Wesley met with men like Cennick, full of servant consciousness of the reality, power and blessedness of Christ's religion; and employing a style, terse from intensity of feeling, and copious from the fullness of the theme – no wonder that, instead of forbidding, he encouraged them to preach the glorious truths which they not merely understood but felt.[18]

Here is confirmation that Cennick's personality was not weak, as had been suggested, but strong and powerful in the cause of preaching Christ. Evangelists of the 18th Century Awakening were not content with a knowledge of the Gospel which remained no more than an intellectual assent to scriptural truths; they felt deeply the impact of the grace of God in their hearts.

Cennick was an example *'par-excellence'* of the preacher who felt deeply because he knew clearly. The message proclaimed had done its life-changing work in his own personality. Charles Wesley expressed this blending of knowledge and feeling perfectly:

> *How can a sinner know*
> *His sins on earth forgiven?*
> *How can my gracious Saviour show*
> *My name inscribed in heaven?*
> *What we have felt and seen*
> *With confidence we tell,*
> *And publish to the sons of men*
> *The signs infallible.*

We who in Christ believe
That he for us hath died,
We all his unknown peace receive,
And feel his blood applied;
Exults our rising soul,
Disburdened of her load,
And swells unutterably full
Of glory and of God.[19]

Both Wesley and Cennick would attribute the assurance in believing and this deep feeling of pardon and liberty to the work of the Holy Spirit. So Wesley continues:

His Spirit to us he gave,
And dwells in us, we know;
The witness in ourselves we have,
And all his fruits we show.[20]

A H Mumford writes:

Cennick was a winning preacher. He did not frighten people with thoughts of judgment and hell. He told them of Christ's love and Heaven. He loved to tell of Naaman's cleansing, of the Good Samaritan and of the Good Shepherd. The country people loved him for his cheerfulness and his message of hope. Nothing could keep them away. When a parish officer threatened the Cennickers (sic) with starvation, the people said, "If you starve us, we will go, and rather than forswear, we will eat grass with the kine".[21]

Mumford is probably right when he says Cennick did not seek to frighten people with judgment and hell, yet there are passages in his published sermons in which he did not draw back from preaching the dire consequences of unbelief and the deliberate rejection of God's grace in Christ. A particularly potent passage occurs in *Village Discourses:*

Who, unregenerate and conscious of his being a natural and carnal man, can do otherwise but shudder when he knows he must die, and after that come to judgment, and when he feels that if he should be called away as he is, he must perish in eternal burnings, and be numbered among foolish virgins, hypocrites, and unbelievers.[22]

But it remains true, as Mumford says, that Cennick's main preaching emphasis is on the powerful love of God in Christ to bring the lost to find salvation; a message of hope and not despair.

In the Preface to the publication of his sermons Cennick explains the focus and purpose of his preaching. He writes:

The subject of these discussions is sincere Christianity, Jesus Christ's Divinity, his eternal existence, his supreme majesty, Incarnation, sufferings and death by which he has saved the world and brought life and immortality to it. The whole collection are simple and plain and suited for sincere people who do not want somewhat curious or diverting but salvation.[23]

By 'sincere Christianity' he meant a message which was not falsified or perverted, free from any impure element. We may question why Cennick did not include the resurrection in his description of sincere Christianity and we shall need to return to this omission. By 'sincere people' he means, not false or pretending, but real and honest. It was people who had a sincere faith, even if it may have been a weak faith, who responded to Cennick's preaching.

At least two of Cennick's published sermons carry a testimonial by George Whitefield. The sermon on *Naaman Cleansed* preached at Bristol in 1743 on the text of 2 Kings 5:13 has this wholehearted commendation by Whitefield:

I have read the following sermon, and like it much...It was preached by a young witness (Cennick was 25 years old) not as yet sent out by imposition of hands from man, but I am persuaded, taught and sent out by God. This sermon is one proof of it...I could give a thousand more, (a rhetorical exaggeration?) and rejoice at this opportunity of publicly acknowledging the preacher of it to be a dear servant of Jesus Christ...May the Lord bless what he has written to thy soul, O reader, whosoever thou art, and incline thee to pray for him, and thy friend and servant in Jesus.[24]

After a typically careful study of Cennick's published works in 1955, Dr Frank Baker produced a valuable handlist of Cennick's writings.[25] This study was to mark the bicentenary of Cennick's death. Dr Baker concluded that the evidence was fairly clear that John Cennick published at least two volumes of collected sermons in 1753-4. The volumes were probably no more than 'bundles' of single sermons bound together.[26] In Cennick's own preface to the first collected edition dated 12 December (Dublin, 1753) he writes, 'Several of these sermons have been published some years ago, and our Saviour has blessed them in the world; may he do the same by the others which are now, or may be added to them...'[27] In the preface to the second collection, also published in Dublin in August 1754, Cennick begins:

> These discourses as well as the former, were written at different Times...Some were taken down by others at the Time of Preaching, but not so accurately that they needed no Correction or Alteration;...and with no other View have I consented to publish them, but to endeavour to spread the Gospel where ever they may come...[28]

Unfortunately, there is no clear evidence as to which sermons were recorded at the time of preaching and afterwards edited, presumably by Cennick. What may be assumed however, is that Cennick was eventually content that the two collections published in 1753-4 fairly represented what he actually preached.

As Baker says, it is a complicated task to make an accurate assessment of the times of the publication of the sermons. Cennick published 34 separate sermons in his lifetime and these, together with a set of six published posthumously, were printed as a set of 40 for about 50 years. It is this corpus of 40 sermons which Couillard has catalogued in his thesis on Cennick's theology (Appendix C)[29] and which is reproduced at the end of this book in a slightly revised form

(Appendix 3). Baker says that he has only discovered three sermons published before 1753, ie. *Naaman Cleansed; The Bloody Issue Healed* and *The Good Samaritan*.[30] As already implied, Cennick was not enthusiastic about the publication of his sermons, and yet, towards the end of his life, he did consent to publishing the two collections which are now available to us. In addition, other collections, selections from the 40, appeared later and at various times.

Of the 40 sermons available for reference, 19 were preached in England, four in the south of Ireland, 12 in the north of Ireland and four in Wales (one is un-located). The published sermons were predominantly from the New Testament. Eight (not seven as in Baker's list) were from Old Testament texts, 21 from the Gospels, two from the Acts of the Apostles, four from St Paul's Epistles and five from the Epistle to the Hebrews. His most frequently used texts therefore, were selected from the Gospels. The Epistles of Peter, James and John were not represented in the published collections.

If, as previous authors have written, Cennick preached once or twice a day, this would mean that over his active ministry from June 1739 to June 1755 he probably preached on 8000-9000 occasions. How many of Cennick's sermons were repeated because of their popularity or success is not known but clearly the 40 selected and published sermons represent only a small fraction of his preaching. Any assessment of his evangelistic work based on published sermons can only therefore be provisional and approximate. We have, nevertheless, considered it to be of interest to examine a selection of 11 sermons, marked * on the schedule in Appendix 3. These were chosen to cover the whole of Cennick's ministry from 1739 to 1755 and the selection includes sermons preached in all the main geographical locations associated with his evangelistic work (with the exception of Wales). They also represent material from both Testaments but chiefly from sermons preached on texts from the Gospels.

Cennick himself accepted that his way of preaching was 'somewhat out of the way of the Church' and expressed his belief that the calling he had received was 'to go a little ahead of the [Moravian] Church' to new places whilst remaining under its direction and care.[31] Podmore writes that the Moravians did have a problem with Cennick's 'activism'. The Moravian Brethren, despite their missionary zeal and activity were somewhat 'passive'. They believed that the Saviour would draw people to himself and their role was to receive converts and make the Saviour known. The Moravians particularly disliked the idea of taking converts from other churches and were ambivalent towards Cennick's 'preaching tours' where a passionate and persuasive evangelism was the order of the day.[32]

Despite Cennick's affectionate relationship to the Moravian Brethren and to Zinzendorf in particular, this did not mean that he was entirely without censure. On his style of preaching, Zinzendorf could scathingly comment that the Moravian pulpits would be dishonoured 'by a boldness which has something theatrical and comedian-like about it.'[33] This rather acerbic assessment of Cennick's preaching may have been a hasty judgment. Other Moravians like Peter Böhler recognised the attraction and popularity of Cennick's way of preaching and expressed some displeasure that members of the Fetter Lane Congregation chose to attend White's Alley to hear Cennick rather than attending the liturgical services at Fetter Lane.[34]

Cennick's style of preaching was typical of 18th Century Revival evangelism. He had, no doubt, heard of Wesley's dictum advocating 'plain truth for plain people'.[35] It may be, as Baker suggests, that Cennick never rose to John Wesley's 'concise vigour' and yet his style was clear, popular and effective. His sermons have a homely, domestic touch; that is they use the every-day domestic language of the 18th Century; though the language is significantly different from that used in succeeding centuries as the style and vocabulary of English prose developed. Cennick's sermons, like those of Whitefield and Wesley, need to be read in the context of a previous era and some effort is needed by the modern mind to appreciate the power of 18th Century preaching. Cennick does not become entangled in complicated sentence structure or highly developed argument, though again, modern readers may find his presentation somewhat tedious.

Cennick's sermon construction is broadly of two types. Some sermons are cast in a narrative form. He takes a biblical 'story' and reconstructs the narrative to suit the thrust of the message he has chosen for the occasion. The narrative style of sermon may have a broadly based structure and the story, as it is retold, is interspersed with both application and appeal. A typical example of this narrative style is the sermon preached at Scholes in Yorkshire in 1752 from the text of John 4:10 and entitled *The Woman of Samaria*. In this sermon Cennick uses a single text to give focus to his message and to provide him with a broadly based structure. The text of John 4:10 is developed using three parts of the verse to give a 'form' to the sermon. He begins by saying that he 'designs to make some observations on the whole history of this conversation of our Saviour with the woman...' The sermon is then developed in a narrative style, retelling the story under the three parts. As an evangelistic message, Cennick eventually deals with the saving work of Christ on the cross, introducing this aspect of his message by moving from the particular words of the woman and applying them to the congregation:

> If you knew who Jesus is, you would ask Him, and he would help you.
>
> If you knew he was The Lord God Almighty, you would think then, Why do I tarry any longer? What though my sins are red like Scarlet, He can make them like Wool, and though they are like Crimson, he can make them like Snow. What horrid Guilt! What cursed Nature can't he wash and make clean? If all the Sins of the World were laid upon one Soul, a single Drop of his Sweat, one precious Drop of his Blood could make him in a Moment fairer than an Angel of God.[36]

Cennick also adopted the more common form of systematically structured sermons where a text was announced and an introduction was followed by clearly defined 'points', exposition, application and appeal. A good example of this homiletic style is to be found in his sermon on Isaiah 38:17 entitled *The Assurance of Faith* preached at Glenevy, Co. Antrim in 1754. The Isaiah text reads, 'Thou hast in love to my soul delivered it from the pit of corruption, for thou hast cast all my sins behind thy back.' This is coupled to a background text from Hebrews 10:22, 'Let us draw near with...full assurance of faith, having our hearts sprinkled from an evil conscience and our bodies washed with pure water,' from which the title of the sermon is taken. After a substantial introductory passage in which Cennick bridges the two Testaments by:

> It is easy to prove out of the Psalms of David and others, as well as out of Isaiah, Ezekiel and Zechariah, that they who believed truly in our Saviour, though so far off, knew their sins were forgiven and blotted out... But there is something particularly beautiful in that writing of *Hezekiah*, out of which I have been reading. It is to me a solid and weighty Account of God's Dealings with him, and tally's (sic) with the Experience of all true Christians in the World.

He then goes on to give the headings under which he proposes to explore and expound the words of Hezekiah, as Cennick describes him, 'the Good King of Israel after a Recovery from sickness, and is a sort of Song of Thanksgiving, and a Relation of his happy Experience, viz. of his own natural Estate, and of the work of Conversion in his Heart'.

The points he makes are typical and illuminating. They are:

(i) The Distress he was in before our Saviour spoke peace to him and delivered him from his sins.

(ii) The Assurance he had of being pardoned, and accepted by his heavenly Father, and saved; and how boldly he testifies that this must be the case with all the Children of God.

(iii) The Cause of it all; which he says was the Love of Jehovah to him – of each of these let me speak a little.

Each of the headings is then expounded.

At the conclusion of the sermon Cennick draws the congregation into an appeal:

> Come ye to the Lamb, and he will ease you; he will undertake for you; he will cast all your sins behind his back, and put a new Song in your Mouth...Ask anything and he will do it for you. Ask then the Forgiveness of

Sins, and to be assured of your eternal Happiness in Him, and you will receive it...Ye shall go to him, and see him whom ye love so much here, and be for ever with him. Amen.[37]

There seems to be no discernible 'development' of homiletic style, or progression of theological presentation between the early sermons of 1739 and those of his later years. It would appear that he quickly found the preaching style and method, probably influenced by Wesley, Whitefield and Harris, which suited his own personality and purposes. As Couillard perceptively writes, '...the times not only created the necessity for, but also elicited the emphasis of his messages'.[38]

Those who have made a careful study of the essential doctrines which Cennick preached have found two rather surprising omissions; the doctrines of sanctification and the resurrection of Christ.

Couillard, in a summary of the major elements of Cennick's doctrinal position, maintains that he emphasises the person of Christ and his essential Divinity, the work of the Holy Spirit and the doctrines of sin and salvation with particular stress on the atonement and salvation by faith alone.[39] It is strange, to say the least, that there is so little importance given to sanctification or the resurrection of Christ. His concern was, of course, to present the gospel in a 'Reformed' cast with the focus on the death of Christ as a propitiation for sin attained only by grace and saving faith in Jesus Christ. He apparently neglected any comparable stress on the resurrection of Christ, without which, as Paul says, preaching and faith are both useless (1 Corinthians 15:14). Neither is there any stress laid on the importance of the demands of a holy life consequent upon salvation by faith. It may be, of course, that Cennick's tendency was to avoid the doctrine of 'scriptural holiness'; so much a part of John Wesley's *raison d'être,* because of the discomfort which Wesley's presentation aroused, especially when expounded by the less able of his preachers. That at least may be understandable even if it is lamentable.

It is, however, less easy to account for Cennick's apparent 'blind spot' of the resurrection of Christ. There are passing references to 'rising again' in his Christological sermons but not the stress on this vital part of the gospel which would be expected by a preacher so committed to the balance of Christian doctrine as presented in the Gospels, Acts of the Apostles and The Epistles. It is even more surprising for a preacher who strongly asserts the indispensable experience of a 'new birth'. Yet Cennick does refer to 'a resurrection for all' in his eschatological views. A passage in his sermon entitled *The First Principles of Christianity* reads, 'That the dead, small and great, just and unjust shall rise again and come to life through the resurrection of Jesus, is fully asserted by St. Paul's first epistle to the Corinthians and our Saviour himself taught it...'[40] This is however, an exceptional passage, rather than a usual one.

V W Couillard, in an admirable summary of Cennick's Christology writes:

> His doctrine of the person and nature of Christ has been found to include such elements as the historical Jesus, the Christ of experience...the incarnation and virgin birth, the two natures, man and God in one person, Christ's mediatorship and high priesthood, and his equality with the Father and the Spirit.[41]

The resurrection is strangely omitted. Referring to Cennick's *Personal Creed* there is again a mysterious neglect of the miraculous rising of Christ from death, so vital to salvation and faith. That perhaps may be explained because the *Personal Creed* was designed to defend biblical Christology and cast in a fashion to confound the Unitarian (Arian) heresy.

The last word on Cennick as a preacher should be those of the preacher himself. In the preface to the 9 August 1754 collection of sermons he writes:

> 'I am sensible the Stile [sic], as well as the Matter, will not divert the Curious with good Language: it is not my Gift; nor have I attempted to dress the plain Doctrines of our Saviour... As far as became a Servant of Christ, I have shunned disputable Points, and only published the general and blessed Doctrines of Salvation by Faith in his Name.'[42]

He might have said of all his preaching, 'It came from God, and it is for God's Glory. It honours Christ and is designed to save sinners.' His chief concern was to point the way to God.

References for Chapter 6

[1] C Podmore, *The Moravian Church in England 1728-1760*, Clarendon Press (Oxford, 1998), pp.50, 88

[2] A Dallimore, *George Whitefield*, Banner of Truth Trust (London, 1970), Vol. 1, p304

[3] *ibid*. Vol. 1, p.305

[4] C Wesley, *The Journal of Rev Charles Wesley MA, The Early Journal, 1736-1739*, Robert Culley (London, 1909), p.232

[5] A Dallimore, *op.cit*. Vol.1, p304, *Letter to John Wesley, citing L Tyerman, John Wesley*, Vol. 1, p.277

[6] *ibid*. Vol. 1, p.305

[7] J E Hutton, *John Cennick: A Sketch*, Moravian Publishing Office (London, 1909), p.60

[8] *ibid*. p.43-44

[9] J H Cooper, *EJJC*, p.36

[10] *ibid*. p.36

[11] *ibid*. p.36

[12] *ibid*. p.38

[13] *ibid*. p.41

[14] *ibid*. p.41

[15] *ibid*. p.41

[16] J Cennick, *An Account of Preaching and Persecution in Wiltshire 1740-1747*, Ref. MS. AB. 98, Moravian Church Archives (London)

[17] G Watson, CA, p.65

[18] V W Couillard, *The Theology of John Wesley, TMHS*, p.98, citing L Tyerman, *The Life and Times of Rev John Wesley*, Vol.1, p.276

[19] F Hildebrandt and O Beckerlegge, eds. *WJWBE*, Vol.7, p.195

[20] *ibid*. p.197

[21] A H Mumford, *Our Church's Story*, Whightman and Co. Ltd. (London, 1911), p.249

[22] J Cennick, *Village Discourses*, p.340, cited V W Couillard, *op.cit.* p.153

[23] J Cennick, *Forty Discourses on Important Subjects*, M Wilks, ed. (London, 1819), Preface by the Author, pp.v-vi

[24] J Cennick, *Naaman Cleansed* (London, 1793), G Whitefield, *To The Reader*, dated 11 March, 1742-3

[25] F Baker, *PWHS*, Vol. xxx, Pts. 2-5

[26] *ibid*. Pt. 4, p.86

[27] *ibid*. Pt. 4, p.86

[28] *ibid*. Pt. 4, p.86

[29] V W Couillard, *op.cit.* pp.215-216

[30] F Baker, *op.cit.* Pt. 3, p.50

[31] C Podmore, *op.cit.* p.197

[32] *ibid*. p.196

[33] *ibid*. p.200

[34] *ibid*. p.200

[35] J Wesley, *Sermons on Several Occasions*, Wesleyan Conference Office (London, 1865), Preface, p.3

[36] J Cennick, *Forty Discourses*, number 33, *The Woman of Samaria*, sermon preached at Scholes, Yorkshire, 1752), see Appendix 3, C21

[37] J Cennick, *Forty Discourses*, number 48, *The Assurance of Faith*, sermon preached at Antrim, 1754), see Appendix 3, C36

[38] V W Couillard, *op.cit.* p.101

[39] *ibid*. p.111

[40] J Cennick, *Forty Discourses*, number 34, *The First Principles of Christianity*, sermon preached in the north of Ireland, 1752) see Appendix 3, C22

[41] V W Couillard, *op.cit.* p.157

[42] F Baker, *op.cit.* Pt. 3, p.51

JOHN CENNICK

Chapter 7

Hymns and Poems
'Now, dear Congregation!'

Children of the Heavenly King
As ye journey, sweetly sing;
Sing your Saviour's worthy praise,
Glorious in his works and ways!

(J R Broome, LHJC, p.218 and J Cennick, *SHCG*, p.66.)

Preface

My Christian family habitually said what we called 'grace' before each meal. 'We thank Thee Lord for this our food; but more because of Jesu's blood. Let manna to our souls be given, the bread of life sent down from heaven'. Little did I know then that those familiar words were my father's adaptation of a grace-verse written by John Cennick for use 'After meat'.[1] At meals taken in our village Wesleyan Methodist Church in South Yorkshire we sang 'grace', 'Be present at our table, Lord; Be here, and everywhere adored; Thy creatures bless, and grant that we May feast in Paradise with thee.' I am sure that few of those worthy Wesleyan folk would have associated the grace we sang so heartily with John Cennick.[2] Neither would they know that the words of Cennick's grace-verse made such a strong appeal to John Wesley that he had them engraved on his family teapot![3] From the early days of his spiritual pilgrimage Cennick's ministry included the composition of about 750 hymns, 151 of which were published on his behalf in 1741. The purposes of this chapter are to trace the Reformation antecedents of Cennick's

113

hymn-writing and to compare his hymns with those of Watts, Wesley and hymn-writers associated with the Moravian Brethren.

Hymns are composed in order to be an essential part of the worship of God by congregations desiring to direct their praise to Him. St Augustine of Hippo writes of a hymn, 'It is a singing to the praise of God. If you praise God, and do not sing, you utter no hymn. If you sing, and praise no God, you utter no hymn. If you praise anything which does not pertain to the praise of God, though in singing you praise, you utter no hymn'.[4] This somewhat convoluted definition reinforces the idea that the essential elements of a hymn are that it should contain praise and that it should be directed to God in the form of singing. The Augustinian definition also serves to draw a distinction between what may be a secular poem set to music and a hymn which is an element of corporate worship. As John Mason Neale writes, 'Church hymns must be the life-expression of all our hearts',[5] the 'heart' being a metonym for the whole person. Hymns are not only recitals of credal truth but are also expressions of Christian devotion to God. J R Watson elaborates:

> Hymns belong primarily to the Church. Since the earliest days of the Christian religion, singing has played a part in Christian worship; hymns assisted in the development of the liturgy of the medieval Church, in the Reformation, and in the Evangelical Revival of the eighteenth century. Hymns permit the congregation to take part actively in a service, and provide a useful if not essential contrast with the other elements of worship.[6]

Excursus

The following excursus establishes the tradition of the psalm-hymn-song in worship during biblical times. It may be omitted by those who choose to move directly to the Reformers and Cennick.

Hymns may well belong primarily to the Christian Church but their origins lie deep within the relationship between Jehovah and His ancient covenant people. The book of *Psalms* is largely a collection of Hebrew religious songs, especially as they were used for worship in the Second Temple. Psalm and Song were composed pieces, often designed for particular occasions. The double title, Psalm and Song, would indicate a poem (eg. by David) which had been popularised, set to music and used in worship. Typical Psalm-Songs are to be found in Psalms 120-134, the so-called *Songs of Ascents.* The *Mishnah* records that fifteen steps led up from the Court of the Women to the Court of the Israelites corresponding to the fifteen Songs of Ascents in the Psalms, and on them the Levites sang. There is no certainty that what they sang was Psalms 120-134 although this has often been assumed and it is at least possible. The most likely reference of the title is to the pilgrimage up to Jerusalem, or the processional ascent of 'the hill of the Lord' (Isaiah 30:29).[7] Hallel, a Hebrew expression describing a Psalm-Song in praise to God is used, for example, with reference to Psalms 113-118 (the Egyptian Hallel). They were used particularly at Passover celebrations, Psalm 113-114 preceding the meal and 115-118 after the last cup was filled. It may even be that these Psalm-Songs were those sung by Jesus and his disciples at the last supper (Mark 14:26).[8] *The Great Hallel* (Psalm 136), with its recurring refrain 'For his love has no end', was particularly fitting for a congregational response, and may have been used in daily synagogue worship services.[9]

A development of the worship praise-song is to be found in the *Song of Zechariah* (Luke 1:68ff) which begins, 'Praise be to the Lord, the God of Israel, because he has come and has redeemed his people'. This follows the even more familiar words of Mary's song, *The Magnificat* (Luke 1:46-55), which opens with words which are hard to better as a praise-song, 'My soul praises the Lord and my spirit rejoices in God my Saviour, for he has been mindful of the humble state of his servant'. Both Zechariah and Mary give expression to exultant joy and praise to God who has 'performed mighty deeds' and 'brought redemption to his people'.

There are undoubted strains of early Christian hymnody woven into Paul's epistles. Perhaps the best example is to be found in Philippians 2:6-11 which concludes, '...and every tongue [shall] confess that Jesus Christ is Lord, to the glory of God the Father'. In Paul's exhortation to the church at Ephesus, he encourages them, 'Speak to one another with psalms, hymns and spiritual songs'. Lest this be misunderstood as merely human intercourse, he continues, 'Sing and make music in your heart to the Lord...' (Ephesians 5:19). Even the serious and sedate James reminds us that singing songs of praise is a legitimate expression of inward happiness! (James 5:13b).

Reformation Roots

The Christian age of the Church Fathers and the medieval period of church history had their own characteristic worship. They are however, largely irrelevant in setting the hymns of Cennick in their historical sequence. During the long period between the 6th Century and the Lutheran Reformation ten centuries later, congregations of worshippers had largely been denied the privileges of participation in worship singing. This changed significantly with Martin Luther (1483-1546) who wrote of his intention, 'to make German psalms for the people, that is spiritual songs, whereby the Word of God may be kept alive among them by singing'.[10] At least one of Luther's mentors, Andreas von Carlstadt (1477-1541), did not share Luther's enthusiasm for psalm singing, and though often brilliant he could also be petty, 'Better one heart-felt prayer than a thousand cantatas... The lascivious notes of the organ awaken thoughts of the world...if there is to be singing, let it be no more than a solo.' 'Relegate organs, trumpets and flutes to the theatre,' he said.[11] Not withstanding von Carlstadt, the year 1524 saw Luther's publication of a hymn book with twenty-three hymns, six of which were based on Psalms; so Luther's people learned to sing as they worshipped.[12] Cennick's hymns also had for their bed-rock both the theology and spirituality of the great German Reformation tradition. The origins of the 16th Century Reformation may well be traced to Luther's disaffection with some Roman Catholic doctrines and practices, but its inspiration gave rise to the use of the Psalms and Christian music in Reformation worship.

Luther's great hymn 'Ein feste Burg ist unser Gott' is an incomparable paraphrase of Psalm 46, 'God is our refuge and strength'. The first verse is following:

A safe stronghold our God is still
A trusty shield and weapon;
He'll help us clear from all the ill
That hath now o'ertaken.
The ancient prince of hell
Hath risen with purpose fell;
Strong mail of craft and power
He weareth in this hour;
On earth is not his fellow.[13]

This hymn, where it is printed in modern hymn books, is translated by Thomas Carlisle (1795-1881), but even so, it would be intellectually and spiritually demanding for a modern congregation. Among other things however, it reminds the singers that they are a part of an assembly that is 'unser Gott', our God who is the strong tower; or as in a later hymn by Isaac Watts, 'God is the refuge of His Saints'.[14] This 'mighty fortress' is not only our safe stronghold, but He is also our sufficient provider. As William Kethe (d.1593?) in his metrical version of Psalm 100 wrote, 'We are His flocke [flock/folk], He doth us feed'.[15] In the early days of the 18th Century Awakening, it is said, this hymn of Kethe's was often sung by congregations on occasions when conversions were celebrated (unconfirmed). Reflections on these themes are not difficult to find in Cennick's own verses. His well known hymn which begins, 'Ere I sleep for every favour...' has this verse:

Thou, my Rock, my Guard, my Tower,
Safely keep,
While I sleep,
Me with all thy Power.[16]

Paul Gerhardt (1607-1676), a Lutheran Pastor, represents German evangelicalism of the 17th Century at its best, hymn writing at its peak, and he ranks alongside Luther. Luther's hymns embraced all the reformation doctrines of grace, atonement and justification in their objective realities. Gerhardt, without losing any reformation doctrinal emphases, wrote his hymns from a more subjective perspective with a style both simple and deeply spiritual. His importance for the story of John Cennick lies in a similarity of style, though it is admitted that Cennick rarely reached the sublime eloquence and genius to be found in Gerhardt. The translations of Paul Gerhardt's hymns by John Wesley is a story to be referred to later, but through Wesley's translation work, the hymns of Gerhardt and other evangelical German hymn writers became known in the early days of the 18th Century Revival. They would be known to John Cennick through his acquaintance both with the Methodists and the Moravians.

Perhaps one of the most treasured of Gerhardt's hymns begins:

Commit thou all thy griefs
And ways into His hands;
To His sure truth and tender care,
Who earth and heaven commands
Who points the clouds their course,
Whom winds and seas obey;
He shall direct thy wandering feet,
He shall prepare thy way.[17]

This superb hymn is believed to have been written by Gerhardt at a particularly stressful time as he was ordered to leave his homeland. In almost total poverty he travelled on foot with his wife and children. Seeking refuge in a village inn, his wife broke down in tears of despair. Gerhardt reminded her of the words, 'Commit thy way unto the Lord' (Psalm 37:5) and retired to write the hymn. Later, in improved circumstances, he presented his wife with the hymn he had written, 'See how God provides! Did I not bid you to trust in God and all would be well?' Even should there be some doubt about the authenticity of the whole story, it probably was written to help his wife in a time of trouble.[18] H A L Jefferson tells us that Gerhardt was designated 'The Wesley of the Fatherland' for there is much in his hymns which is later to be found in the hymns of Charles Wesley.[19] Gerhardt was the author of over 120 hymns, almost all of them combining the simplicity of the Gospel with the depth of unshakeable faith in the providence of God. We have not found any Cennick verses to compare with the best of Gerhardt although it is not difficult to discern Cennick's simple trust in God, even in the most difficult of times. An example of Cennick on a favoured theme is found in a hymn he entitled *For Charity (Love):*

> *Thou Lord, my God, art love*
> *In thee I live, and move;*
> *Teach me all thy property,*
> *Learn [sic] me how to walk with thee;*
> *Meek, and lowly, as my Lord;*
> *True, and faithful, as his word.*[20]

The theme may echo that of Gerhardt but the poetic quality is hardly equal. For the very best of Paul Gerhardt, the reader is recommended to ponder the beauty and the dedication of his hymn which contains these two profoundly moving verses:

> *Jesu, Thy boundless love to me*
> *No thought can reach, no tongue declare;*
> *O, knit my thankful heart to Thee,*
> *And reign without a rival there.*
> *Thine wholly, Thine alone, I am,*
> *Be Thou alone my constant flame.*
>
> *O love, how cheering is Thy ray;*
> *All pain before Thy presence flies;*
> *Care, anguish, sorrow, melt away*
> *Where'er Thy healing beams arise:*
> *O Jesu, nothing may I see,*
> *Nothing desire, or seek, but Thee.*[21]

John Cennick in one of his best hymns can reflect on the same theme; but with diminished grandeur?

> *O Lord, my God! Whose sovereign love*
> *Is still the same, not e'er can move;*
> *Look to the covenant, and see*
> *For once thy love was shown to me;*
> *Consider, O my dearest friend,*
> *And love [me] always to the end.*[22]

119

Paul Gerhardt was apparently attracted by the then unusual 8336 metre. His own hymn was on his heart and lips when he passed to his eternal reward in 1676:

> *Death can never kill us even,*
> *but relief*
> *from all grief*
> *to us then is given.*[23]

On this occasion, using the same metre, Cennick can equal the great Gerhardt:

> *So, when e're in death I slumber*
> *Let me rise*
> *With the wise,*
> *Counted in their number.*[24]

It may be said, with some degree of confidence, that this Cennick hymn previously referred to with its well known opening line, 'Ere I sleep, for every favour...' is amongst the best dozen hymns he ever wrote and thoroughly deserved its popularity, at least until modern times.

From Watts to Cennick

The 17th Century was hugely influential in paving the way for the popularity of the hymn-singing which was to prove such a vital element of the 18th Century Revival. It was from the background of Puritan England and from the period of dissent that the young Isaac Watts (1674-1748) was to emerge as a prolific pioneer of hymn-writing. Watts was an Independent (or Congregationalist). He had been strongly opposed to hymn-singing as part of public Christian worship. As Jefferson says, 'It is fairly certain that when Watts began his work, congregational hymn singing was restricted to a few isolated churches.'[25] Worship singing had usually been in the form of metrical psalms, a feature of Christian worship stretching back over many centuries. The reciting of Psalms was a feature of Roman Catholic monasteries and convents throughout the continent of Europe. In the Calvinistic Reformed Churches, the influence of which was strongly felt in England's Puritan tradition, the Psalter was the only form of congregational singing reckoned to be sanctioned by scripture.[26] It was in this rather solid and unemotional ocean of congregational psalm-singing that Isaac Watts began to write a different genre of worship hymns. Watts was a scholarly as well as a deeply spiritual man. His birth date coincided with the repeal of the Declaration of Indulgence which granted a degree of toleration for the non-conformist constituency. Isaac Watts' father, a deacon in an Independent Church in Southampton, was imprisoned, during which time Mrs Watts, with young Isaac, watched and waited outside the gates of the prison for her beloved husband to be released. In order to further his modest education, the bright boy of the Watts family entered an academy at Stoke Newington. As a young man of twenty, Isaac Watts penned his first hymns, in some measure to respond to his father's challenge to provide a better alternative to the often dreary fare available at that time.[27] The first of Watts' 'new' hymns began:

> *Behold the glories of the Lamb*
> *Before His Father's throne;*
> *Prepare new honours for His name,*
> *And songs before unknown.*[28]

The last line was surely, if unwittingly, prophetic. After that initial attempt he wrote hymns with remarkable regularity. The two principal collections of Watts' hymns were *Hymns and Spiritual Songs* (1707) and *The Psalms of David* (1719).[29] Both were to become popular and useful in Independent Congregations.

It would not be within the scope of this chapter to enlarge on the importance of Watts as a pioneer in the genre of hymns which were to become such an integral part of the 18th Century Awakening. What is important, as we move into that revival period with its magnificent proliferation of high quality hymnology, is to say that only Charles Wesley could consistently match the erudition and profound evangelical spirituality which was to be found in Watts at his best. Millar Patrick writes, 'Watts saw with the clear intuition of genius what needed to be done and alone he did it.' All who came afterwards, even when they excel him, are his debtors.[30]

Of Cennick's contemporaries, there were none so influential in the hymn-writing for public worship as the Methodists and the Moravians, represented by the Wesleys and Zinzendorf. John Wesley's translations of hymns from the German language began in 1735 when the Wesley brothers found themselves in the providence of God, sailing with a group of Moravian brethren on the *Simmonds* bound for Georgia. A particularly stormy passage brought the Wesleys, their English companions and the Moravians together. The violence of the storm caused no anxiety to the Brethren. In contrast the Wesley contingent were fearful for their lives. The source of the peace, so apparent in the demeanour of the Moravians, intrigued John Wesley, and the consequent companionship led him to learn the German language so that he could communicate more easily with the Moravian Brethren. There is an interesting mention of this important event in one of Wesley's sermons (Sermon 117 *On Knowing Christ after the Flesh* preached from 2 Corinthians 5:16 in Plymouth on 15 August 1789):

> It was between fifty and sixty years ago, that, by the gracious providence of God, my brother and I, in our voyage to America, became acquainted with the (so-called) Moravian Brethren. We quickly took knowledge what spirit they were of; six and twenty of them being in the same ship with us. We not only contracted much esteem, but a strong affection for them....I translated many of their hymns, for the use of our own congregations.[31]

The publication of Wesley's first collection of sacred songs, *Psalms and Hymns,* was printed in Charleston, South Carolina in 1737. Nuelson comments:

> This collection is remarkable in several respects. It is the oldest hymn book published by an Anglican clergyman for the use of Anglican congregations. Further, it is the first hymn book published in America. And this oldest American-Anglican hymn book contains among its 78 hymns, five which were translated by John Wesley from the German.[32]

Thus Wesley opened the chapter on English hymn-singing which flowered in the Revival. In 1738 there appeared a second *Collection of Psalms and Hymns* which contained five more translations of German hymns. Eventually, John Wesley translated a total of 33 hymns from the German language, all produced in the eventful stay in Georgia from 6 February 1736 to 2 December 1737, and all before the remarkable evangelical experience in Aldersgate Street in 1738.[33] Wesley often refers to these translations; 'German verse', 'translated German', 'made verses', and so on.[34]

The 1780 *Collection of Hymns for the Use of the People Called Methodists* contained some of the finest hymns of Gerhard Tersteegen.[35] It is not difficult to imagine how Tersteegen's hymns would appeal to the mystic element in Wesley's temperament. Gerhard Tersteegen (1697-1769) was a German mystic of pure spirituality and evangelical faith. One hymn in particular appealed to Wesley and he translated this to make it available to English-speaking congregations:

> *Thou hidden love of God, whose height,*
> *Whose depth unfathomed, no man knows;*
> *I see from far thy beauteous light,*
> *Inly I sigh for thy repose;*
> *My heart is pained, nor can it be*
> *At rest, till it finds rest in thee.*[36]

This hymn was judged by two American critics, Emerson and Wendell Holmes, to be the greatest hymn in the English language. Different critics, of course, assign this distinction to other hymns.[37]

The importance of the Wesley translations of German hymns for the John Cennick story is that they would be available to him in the formative years of his spiritual pilgrimage both from his contact with the Wesleys and from his association with the Moravian Brethren at Marienborn and Herrnhaag. There, a considerable corpus of German hymnology was available, including the works of Zinzendorf himself. The well known Zinzendorf hymn:

> *Jesu, Thy blood and righteousness*
> *My beauty are my glorious dress;*

Midst flaming worlds in these array'd,
With joy shall I lift up my head.[38]

reflects almost perfectly the spiritual tone of some of Cennick's hymns; for example, Cennick could write:

Joy seized my heart, amazed I stood;
When lo! in garments rolled in blood,
Jesus, my Lord, before me stands,
My name was graven on his hands.[39]

The reader will judge the respective merits of Zinzendorf and Cennick, though both verses do avoid the more bizarre vocabulary of the Moravian 'Blood and Wounds' theology.

To return now to the Methodist influence on Cennick. Bernard Lord Manning, a scholarly Congregationalist in his well known work *The Hymns of Wesley and Watts,* wrote that the *Collection of Hymns for the People called Methodist* published in 1780 by John and Charles Wesley, '...ranks in Christian literature with the Psalms, the Book of Common Prayer...In its own way it is perfect, unapproachable, elemental in its perfection. You cannot alter it except to mar it; it is a work of supreme devotional art by a religious genius.'[40] One may recognise the rhetorical extravagance, but it has to be examined in its entirety if one is to maintain a critical spirit. It was this same *Collection of Hymns* which carried the famous *Preface*, written by John Wesley, in which he describes the collection of almost entirely his brother's hymns as, 'a little body of experimental and practical divinity'.[41] So, this volume of originally 525 hymns was the crowning glory of Wesleyan hymn-writing and probably the most lasting production of hymnology which inspired and was inspired by the deep work of the Spirit of God on the waters of darkest England between 1738 and the end of that century. This famous collection of hymns of the Revival had been preceded by others produced in the years immediately following the personal awakening of Charles Wesley at Whitsuntide 1738. The life changing experience of the younger Wesley opened the flood-gates of pent-up spiritual and evangelical hymnody. Important 'collections' of hymns followed in four successive years from 1739-1742; all of them available to the societies of new converts during the early active years of John Cennick's life and work. Charles Wesley became the natural successor to Isaac Watts. His first hymn was written to celebrate his conversion:

> *Where shall my wond'ring soul begin?*
> *How shall I all to heaven aspire?*
> *A slave redeemed from death and sin,*
> *A brand plucked from eternal fire,*
> *How shall I equal triumphs raise,*
> *Or sing my great Deliverer's praise?*[42]

This hymn is very probably that to which Charles Wesley referred to in his *Journal* for Tuesday, May 23, 1738; 'At nine I began an hymn upon my conversion, but was persuaded to break off for fear of pride. Mr Bray coming encouraged me to proceed in spite of Satan. I prayed Christ to stand by me, and finished the hymn.'[43]

Year after year from the pen of Charles Wesley poured several thousand hymns which were used as an important element of worship but also as a means of educating the 'common people' in the biblical doctrines of the Revival. It is not the purpose of this chapter to expound in detail the history, theology or impact of Wesleyan hymns; only to serve as a reminder of one of the formative influences on Cennick's spiritual experience and the encouragement and model they must have been for his own hymn compositions. Manning comments:

> The greatness of Wesley's hymns lies in the exactness with which they recapture and represent the life in the New Testament. In them, as in it, we move high above all ecclesiastical divisions and out of hearing of almost all theological controversies. Wesley speaks the language of the Gospels and the Epistles.[44]

The same may be said for the majority of hymns penned by Cennick, but perhaps without the stately metres and polished verse of Wesley. Cennick was expressive, sometimes rugged and vividly descriptive.

Although most of the Wesley hymns portray the spiritual experience of a 'heart set free', there is one element which recurs and over-arches all others. It is the note of happy assurance of faith, a confidence in God expressed by John Wesley in his last moments, 'Best of all, God is with us'. Wesley's hymns redound with his own confidence in the personal salvation, 'which God supplies through his eternal Son'; a salvation accomplished on the cross and appropriated by trust in Christ. This same objective salvation, expressed in a subjective biblical vocabulary and which never ventures too far from blood-bought redemption lies at the heart of almost all Cennick wrote; and this Wesley would have endorsed in ringing approval. Cennick could write:

> *Thou, who suffer'dst once for all,*
> *Thou just, and holy one.*
> *For a friendless criminal,*
> *O! let thy blood atone!*
> *Grant me strength, and change my will,*
> *And henceforth thee to please I'll strive;*
> *My backslidings freely heal,*
> *And all my sin forgive!*[45]

This particular verse has not been selected because it can compare favourably with Wesley, or because it represents the best of Cennick, but because it gives expression to his experience of the sacrifice of Christ. Wesley could reflect Cennick perhaps in superior verses:

> *O love divine! What hast thou done!*
> *Th' immortal God hath died for me!*
> *The Father's co-eternal Son*
> *Bore all my sins upon the tree;*
> *Th' immortal God for me hath died,*
> *My Lord, my Love is crucified.*

> *Is crucified for me and you,*
> *To bring us rebels back to God:*
> *Believe, believe the record true,*
> *Ye all are bought with Jesu's blood;*
> *Pardon for all flows from his side;*
> *My Lord, my Love is crucified.*[46]

A second advent hymn, which has retained its popularity since its original version was penned by Cennick, is now more often sung to a Charles Wesley adaptation. Cennick's first verse is:

> *Lo! He cometh, countless Trumpets,*
> *Blow before his bloody Sign!*
> *Midst ten Thousand Saints and Angels,*
> *See the Crucified shine,*
> *Allelujah! Welcome, welcome bleeding Lamb!*[47]

The reader will detect a little Moravian luridness in these lines and it is not surprising that Charles Wesley, although attracted to the hymn in its original form, modified it without significantly changing the second advent theology. So Wesley writes:

> *Lo! He comes with clouds descending,*
> *Once for favour'd sinners slain!*
> *Thousand thousand saints attending*
> *Swell the triumph of his train:*
> *Hallelujah!*
> *God appears on earth to reign!*[48]

If John Cennick often echoed the hymns of the Wesleys, he was surely equally influenced by his admiration for those of the Moravian Brethren, especially the hymns of Zinzendorf. *In The Dictionary of Hymnology,* Julian comments:

> The key note of Zinzendorf's hymns and of his religious character was the deep and earnest personal devotion to and fellowship with the crucified Saviour...Many of his hymns are worthy of note and are distinguished by a certain noble simplicity...unshaken faith in the reconciling grace of Christ, entire self-consecration, willingness to spend and to be spent in the Master's service, and fervent brotherly love.[49]

This is a typical Zinzendorf verse:

> *I thirst, Thou wounded Lamb of God*
> *To wash me in Thy cleansing blood,*

> *To dwell within Thy wounds; then pain*
> *Is sweet, and life or death is gain.*[50]

There is a familiar Moravian reference to the sacrificial death of Christ cast in the vocabulary of blood shed and wounds suffered. George Whitefield writing to the Moravians in 1753 quaintly expresses this view: '[There were]...a whole ferago of superstitious, not to say idolatrous fopperies introduced into the English Nation'.[51] But Zinzendorf in particular could also be admirably restrained as he was in the verse above. This emphasis is less conspicuous in Cennick although echoes of Zinzendorf are to be found. An example of Cennick in a Love Feast hymn reads:

> *Jesus, the Lamb, for sinners slain,*
> *The saints' eternal food;*
> *Give us thy flesh to eat today,*
> *And let us drink thy blood.*
> *Come, Prince of Peace, in glory come,*
> *All prejudice remove;*
> *O come, and all our hearts prepare*
> *To keep the feast of love!*[52]

If this is not quite the language which some modern minds can easily sing, it clearly alludes to the words of Jesus himself (John 6:53-54). Peter Gubi writes, 'Having made the statement that Cennick's language was influenced by the Moravians, it is interesting to note that in many of the hymns written by him the language bears a remarkable resemblance...to that used at Herrnhaag'.[53] Zinzendorf can pen these inspiring words of confidence in the death and righteousness of Christ:

> *Bold shall I stand in Thy great day;*
> *For who ought to my charge shall lay?*
> *Fully absolved through these I am,*
> *From sin and fear, from guilt and shame.*[54]

('through these', that is, through the Saviour's blood and righteousness). Cennick's own verse which begins with a double interrogative, 'How shall I come before the Lord! Or bow before his throne?' and answers:

> *Lo! then in JESUS I presume,*
> *The Lamb of sinners slain;*
> *Boldly in Jesus' name I come,*
> *And look with him to reign.*
>
> *Behold! Amidst her faithful sons,*
> *I come before my LORD!*
> *I come in Jesus' righteousness*
> *And wait for his reward.*[55]

It may be that Cennick cannot quite match the eloquence of Zinzendorf, but their theology and experience are perfectly in tune.

The sub-title of this chapter, 'Now, dear Congregation!' is unusual in that it appears that the hymn is addressed to the congregation rather than to God. In fact the hymn is an invitation to the congregation to view the Lamb, his passion and his headship over the Church and to find rest in the Saviour. This three verse, nine line hymn, in Watson's view is a very Moravian hymn and is attributed to Cennick on the basis of John Newton's hand-written annotations on his own copy.[56]

James Montgomery (1771-1854) owed a great deal to the influence of Cennick and the Moravians. Rev John Montgomery and his wife, James' parents, were born in Scotland, but for a period of years were associated with the Gracehill Moravian settlement in the Ahogill area of Co. Antrim, established as a consequence of John Cennick's successful evangelistic preaching. John Montgomery was converted to Christ as a result of Cennick's preaching. James Montgomery was educated at Gracehill and Fulneck by the Moravians and was to become a nationally known and popular poet, hymn-writer, editor of a Sheffield weekly newspaper, an ardent pioneer of the Sunday School movement and supporter of numerous philanthropic causes.[57]

The hymns of John Cennick were saturated with Scripture references and allusions typical of the new genre of worship singing which began with Isaac Watts. Some of Cennick's hymns are 'sermons in verse'. He has titles which indicate the 'text', for example:

I Press towards the Mark;
Follow thou Me;
I deserve to know Nothing but Christ;
Faithful is He that hath Promised.

Other titles indicate biblical 'themes':

The Marriage of the Lamb;
The Love of God;
To the Majesty of God;
The Triumph of the Church.

There are titles which indicate a 'subjective experience':

For Perseverance;
The Distress of Spirit;
Rejoicing;
Under Convictions.

Another group of hymns, the content of which is indicated in the title are 'hymns for occasions':

Sunday Morning;
Before Sacrament;
After Sermon;
At Parting from Friends.

A further format used by Cennick is 'dialogue verses' where the congregation of male and female respond alternately; for example, *Adding to the Church* where six verses are sung in unison, men sing verses 7-8; women sing verses 9-10 and all complete the hymn with verses 11-14.[58] A more usual example is entitled, *In a Dialogue between men and women; composed for the Society at Kingswood* based on Ephesians 5:19. In this hymn all 18 verses are divided into two parts, one for men with responsive lines for women.[59]

As the hymns of John Cennick are read alongside those of Charles Wesley, there are some interesting parallels to be found. A few selected examples will suffice to illustrate the similarity of expression occurring in the two writers:

(i) *Arise, my soul, arise,*
Thy Saviour's sacrifice! (Wesley, 1742)

Arise! my soul, arise!
And view the Almighty's throne... (Cennick, 1741)

(ii) *Captain of Israel's Host, and guide*
Of all who seek the land above... (Wesley, 1762)

Captain of the hosts above
Prepare our dangerous way. (Cennick, 1741)

(iii) *Leave no unguarded place,*
No weakness of the Soul... (Wesley, 1749)

Let no unguarded word
Offend my gracious Lord! (Cennick, 1741)

(iv) *A slave redeemed from death and sin,*
A brand plucked from eternal fire. (Wesley, 1739)

Thus from an infant have I been
A brand prepared to burn in hell (Cennick, 1741)

and finally,

(v) *Leader of faithful souls, and guide*
Of all that travel to the sky... (Wesley, 1747)

Leader of Jacob, Israel's guide,
Be thou my light, my way! (Cennick, 1741)

These examples, and there are others, do no more than indicate that certain particular language ideas were common to the two authors. Their inter-dependency is not to be inferred as insufficient information is available to make such a connection.

Cennick's Hymn Collections

We are again indebted to the careful and comprehensive research by Dr Frank Baker for a concise survey of John Cennick's published hymns.[60] Cennick's first literary production was a volume of hymns and it is on his hymns that, it is said, his fame chiefly rests. The authors have a different view, believing that Cennick's contribution to the Revival was focused rather more on his evangelistic preaching than on his hymns. As we have already indicated Cennick rarely reached the supreme heights of spiritual genius displayed by Isaac Watts and Charles Wesley and it is to be conceded that Cennick's compositions are often common-place by comparison. Yet he composed freely and helpfully for his congregations until he had 750 hymns and poems credited to him, although many of them are buried in 18th Century religious history.

His first published volume is entitled, *Sacred Hymns for the Children of God in the Days of their Pilgrimage*. This collection was printed in London and sold by B Millers in Houndsditch, Bishopgate (sic) in 1741. Thus Cennick was but a youth of 23 years, the time of his separation from the Wesleys, when 151 of his early hymns were published. This first collection has an autobiographical preface in which Cennick writes of his early life and struggles and his coming into the assurance of faith in Christ as his Saviour. The 1741 collection was followed by a 'Second Edition' in which there are 152 hymns with an alphabetical index. A series of collections followed with the title *Sacred Hymns for the use of Religious Societies* which included some 'dialogue' hymns and were issued by Felix Farley in 1763. These contained 39 numbered hymns not previously published, and this volume was reprinted in Bristol and London in 1770. Similar volumes with various titles and with differing contents had been published previously in 1745 and 1747.[61]

In 1754, *The Divine Musical Miscellany, being a Collection of Psalms and Hymn Tunes* appeared, printed by R Williamson and sold at John Morgan's in Half Moon Alley, the third house from Bishopsgate Street! Many of the tunes are specially composed for Cennick's various collections. The *Miscellany* was prepared for use in Whitefield's Tabernacle, London, where Cennick had, in earlier years, conducted hymn-singing classes, but there is no suggestion that it was actually prepared by him. The *Miscellany* has an 11 page introduction on the elements of music.[62] Finally, his *Nunc dimittis* (see Luke 2:29) which is described as 'some lines of the Reverend Mr Cennick (who departed this life July 4 1755) which he wrote some time ago, and carried with him in his Pocket-Book, where they were found after his decease.' (London, 1755).[63] Two further collections were to appear. *A Collection of Hymns of the Children of God in all ages, from the beginning till now* (in two parts). This volume was designed chiefly for the use of the congregations in union with the Brethren Church. It was published in London (1754) and was to be available at all the Brethren's Chapels. The Preface refers to, 'recent and well known' hymn-writers such as Dr Watts, Stennet, Davis, Erskine, Wesley, Cennick, etc.[64] In 1789, *A Collection of Hymns for the use of the Protestant Church of the United Brethren...* was printed in London and sold at the Brethren's Chapels in Great Britain and Ireland.[65]

References for Chapter 7

[1]   J R Broome, ed. *LHJC*, p.181

[2]   *ibid*. p.180

[3]   F Baker, *PWHS*, Vol. xxx, Pt. 2, p.41

[4]   J R Watson, *The English Hymn: A Critical and Historical Study*, OUP (Oxford, 1999), p.2, citing J Julian, *A Dictionary of Hymnology* (London, 1892), p.640

[5]   *ibid*. p.4, citing John Mason Neale, *Hymns of the Eastern Church* (London, 1984), p.xvii

[6]   *ibid*. p.8

[7]   D Kidner, Psalms 1-72, *Tyndale Old Testament Commentaries*, Inter Varsity Press (London, 1973), p.43

[8]   D Kidner, Psalms 73-150, Tyndale *Old Testament Commentaries,* Inter Varsity Press (London, 1973), p.401

[9]   *ibid*. p.457

[10] E Houghton, *Christian Hymn-Writers*, Evangelical Press of Wales (Bridgend, 1982), p.20

[11] R Bainton, *Here I Stand*, Lion (Tring, 1978), p.208

[12] *ibid*. p.345

[13] J R Watson, *op.cit.* p.42, see *MHBL*, number 319, and *MHB*, number 494

[14] *ibid*. p.42

[15] J Telford, *The Methodist Hymn Book Illustrated in History and Experience*, Epworth Press (London, 1934), p.4

[16] J Cennick, *SHCG,* pp.78-79, see G Watson, *CA*, p.55, and J R Broome, *op.cit.* p.17

[17] J L Nuelson, *John Wesley and the German Hymn* (Calverly, Yorkshire, 1972), pp.129-130, see *MHBL,* number 20, and *MHB*, number 507

[18] E Houghton, *op.cit.* p.27

[19] H A L Jefferson, *Hymns in Christian Worship*, Rockliff (London, 1950), p.137

[20] J Cennick, *op.cit.* p.123, see J R Broome, *op.cit.* p.106

[21] J L Nuelson, *op.cit.* pp.131-132, see *MHBL*, number 143, and *MHB*, number 430 <u>Note</u>: Nuelson (p.48), confirms that this Gerhardt hymn was translated by J Wesley in 1738 and first published by him in 1739. The whole hymn of 16 six-line verses is to be found in Nuelson, pp.131-135; 4 verses only are printed in *MHB*, number 430, and 5 verses only in *MHBL*, number 143.

[22] J Cennick, *op.cit.* p.93 (omits 'me'), see J R Broome, *op.cit.* p.198

[23] F Cook, *Our Hymn-Writers and their Hymns*, Evangelical Press (Darlington, 2005), p.24

[24] J Cennick, *op.cit.* pp.78-79, see G Watson, *op.cit.* p.56, and J R Broome, *op.cit.* p.17

[25] H A L Jefferson, *op.cit.* p.42

[26] *ibid.* p.43

[27] *ibid.* pp.46-47

[28] *ibid.* p.47

[29] J D Douglas, ed. *NIDCC*, p.1031

[30] E Houghton, *op.cit.* p.54

[31] H A L Jefferson, *op.cit.* p.135, *J Wesley, Sermons on Several Occasions*, Sermon cxvii, *On Knowing Christ after the Flesh*, para. 8

[32] J L Nuelson, *op.cit.* p.9

[33] *ibid.* p.9

[34] H A L Jefferson, *op.cit.* p.136

[35] J R Watson, *op.cit.* p.209

[36] F Hildebrandt and O Beckerlegge, eds. *WJWBE*, Vol. 7, p.491

[37] H A L Jefferson, *op.cit.* p.144

Note: The whole of Tersteegen's hymn of 8 six-line verses is to be found in Nuelson, pp.119-120; *MHB,* number 433 has 6 verses, and *MHBL,* number 208 has 4 verses.

[38] J L Nuelson, *op.cit.* p.153, see *MHB*, number 370

[39] J R Broome, *op.cit.* p.129, J Cennick, *SHCG*, p.151

[40] B L Manning, *The Hymns of Wesley and Watts*, Epworth Press (London, 1948), p.14

[41] MHB, Preface

[42] F Hildebrandt and O Beckerlegge, *op.cit.* p.116

[43] *ibid.* pp.116-117
Note: The whole hymn of 7 verses may be found in *WJWBE,* Vol. 7, pp.116-117, *MHB* number 361 has 5 verses only.

[44] B L Manning, *op.cit.* p.86

[45] J R Broome, *op.cit.* p.86

[46] F Hildebrandt and O Beckerlegge, *op.cit.* p.114
Note: The same features of objective doctrine and personal experience, the same pleading tones pervade the two hymns. They may be found in J R Broome, *LHJC*, number 65, pp.85-86 and *MHB,* number 186. It is not suggested that one writer was dependant on the other, but that both hearts beat as one.

[47] G Watson, *CA,* p.87, see *MHBL*, number 133 (adapted)

[48] J Telford, *op.cit.* p.151
Note: This hymn is commented on helpfully in G Watson, *CA,* pp.23, 87, 109-111. The Wesley version is found in *MHB*, number 264 where it is regretfully attributed to Charles Wesley alone without reference to John Cennick. A Moravian version is printed in *MHBL*, number 133. The popularity of the distinctive advent hymn is probably aided by the fine tune 'Hemsley' composed by Thomas Olivers, one of Wesley's early preachers, though it may be sung with equal success to the Welsh tune 'Cwm Rhondda'.

[49] E Houghton, *op.cit.* pp.74-75

[50] J L Nuelson, *op.cit.* p.146, see E Houghton, *ibid.* p.75

[51] A Dallimore, *George Whitefield*, Vol. 2, p.331, citing Whitefield's Works (London and Edinburgh, 1771), Vol. 4, p.254

[52] J R Broome, *op.cit.* p.44

[53] P Gubi, *Whither John Cennick*, MA Dissertation (University of Bristol, 1998), p.33

[54] F Hildebrandt and O Beckerlegge, *op.cit.* p.310, see *MHB*, number 370

[55] J R Broome, *op.cit.* pp.2-3, J Cennick, *op.cit.* p.2

[56] G Watson, *op.cit.* pp.66, 106

[57] J Pagdin, Lecture, James Mongomery, Raikes Historical Society (Sheffield, 1964)

[58] J R Broome, *op.cit.* pp.151-153, J Cennick, *op.cit.* p.181

[59] *ibid.* p.177, *ibid.* pp.186-187

[60] F Baker, *op.cit.* Pt. 2, pp.40-44

[61] *ibid.* pp.41-43

[62] *ibid.* p.43

[63] *ibid.* p.43

[64] *ibid.* p.44

[65] *ibid.* p.44
Note: This summary of Hymn and Psalm collections associated with J Cennick is taken from F Baker, *PWHS*, Pt. 2. The information has been included in this chapter for those who wish to read more widely and because, so far as is known, the details of Cennick's hymn collections has not been published so comprehensively elsewhere.

JOHN CENNICK

Chapter 8

Cennick for Today
'Paul Revived - Again'

The comforts, and the hopes, and peace,
Which I, at times, receive,
Shall never make my cravings cease,
Till thou thy kingdom give:
O let me to thy kingdom come,
And share thy purity;
O Lord, delay not, take me home,
I long to be with thee.

(From a hymn entitled *Longing for Glory - The Same,*
J R Broome, LHJC, p.191 and J Cennick, SHCG, p.207.)

Prologue

History, we are often reminded, is really 'His story', a record of the activity of the God of infinity and eternity in the realm of space and time. As such, it is a living thing. History, to be true to itself, must never be a mere chronicle of the long-ago, a collection of facts to inform the reader or listener. History must not only inform but inspire. Its data should not merely throw light on the past, but generate faith and clarity of vision for the future. That is especially true when studying the lives of those individuals whom God has used in shaping the events of the past. In the case of Christians, their work was service for the Kingdom of God on earth, and that is a living, ongoing Kingdom in which all Christians are called to serve. We

139

therefore need to draw upon the annals of Christian service to give us in the present a better understanding of divine possibilities and the extraordinary promises of grace so that our own endeavours may be more effective in achieving God's purposes through our own lives.

This account of the life and work of John Cennick has sought to put him in the context of his own times and contemporaries, but it would be incomplete if it did not also make some effort to put him in the context of our own times, with life as it is today. This final chapter, therefore, will aim to make Cennick's life relevant by firstly drawing attention to the places associated with him where those who have a mind to do so may draw inspiration, and secondly by pointing out the several ways in which his example may profitably be applied to gospel work and worship in the present age, in which sin and unbelief loom as large as they did in his. What worked for him may not work for us, but the Holy Spirit is still available to guide and enable us.

On the Cennick Trail

Bearing in mind the brevity of Cennick's life and that he did not attain to national fame in his lifetime, the number of places associated with him still in existence is quite considerable.

In his home town of Reading, the ancient parish church of St Lawrence, built in the perpendicular style, where he first found peace with God, still stands in the town centre adjacent to the old Town Hall. It is still in regular use for worship and for youth work, though unfortunately not open to the public other than at service times. The Cennick family home is understood to have been located in the same street, but there is nothing now remaining of it and local attempts to have a commemorative plaque displayed on the site have so far been unavailing. Also to be seen from Forbury Road are the ruins of the Benedictine abbey which Cennick used to frequent during his teenage years of despair and spiritual distress leading to his conversion.

In Kingswood, three miles east of Bristol, the scene of Cennick's labours as an associate of both John Wesley and George Whitefield, he is remembered in a road named Cennick Avenue. Until ten years ago a tree known as Cennick's Tree (or possibly one grown from it) stood in the grounds of Kingswood Moravian Church in Regent Street at the corner of Moravian Road, on the site where he preached his first sermon. The present church was opened in 1857 to mark the centenary of the original one of 1757 which was built to house the congregation remaining after Cennick's split from Whitefield and the latter's repossession of his Kingswood 'Tabernacle'. Since 1992 it has also been home to the local United Reformed Church, the direct descendent of Whitefield's 'Tabernacle' congregation; a nice touch of reconciliation and reunion two centuries on!

The old Whitefield Tabernacle in Park Road, Kingswood, built under Cennick's direction in 1742, still stands but has been very badly damaged by vandalism and arson and is now in a state of dilapidation. It featured a few years ago in the BBC2 television 'Restoration' series but unfortunately failed to attract funding and is probably now beyond restoration anyway.

Between Kingswood and Hanham stands Mount Hill, on which in 1951 the local council established a memorial to the work of Wesley and Whitefield who both used it as a convenient open-air auditorium, 'a meadow on the top of a hill' as Wesley called it.[1] It also commemorates persecuted Baptist preachers who held services in the woods thereabouts even before them. The monument features a 65 feet high electric beacon showing a green light at night-time which can be seen for some miles around. Whether Cennick also preached at the same spot is not known for certain but there is every likelihood that he would have done so, especially because the place is often referred to as Hanham Mount, as it was even in Wesley's day.[2] Cennick listed Hanham among the preaching places he used during 1739-40 when he was working with the Wesleys.[3] A replica of the pulpit from the Colliers' School in which he was employed stands on the hilltop site; the original has been preserved and restored and is kept at the present Kingswood School in Lansdown, Bath. The site of the old school itself is still marked by a plate on one of the buildings of the present training school in Britannia Road, Kingswood, which occupies it now.

In Wiltshire, the real launch pad of Cennick's campaign of evangelism was Castle Combe, eight miles north-east of Bath. This picturesque village, with its church, village cross and stream flowing down the centre of the main street, still looks very much as it would have done in his day. It is intriguing to visualise the scenes of revival that took place there as the fervent young preacher proclaimed the Gospel to crowds drawn from this and neighbouring villages.

At East Tytherton, near Chippenham, Cennick's house and adjoining chapel still stands and is used for Moravian worship and as the home of a retired Moravian minister (Rev Peter Gubi). The chapel contains a communion table and chair made from the wood of a tree under which Cennick used to preach in a nearby orchard. Behind the house stands another building known as Kalloway's House, formerly a boarding school, which had a connecting corridor into the manse. Apart from this and Malmesbury, established in 1770, Swindon is the only other place in Wiltshire that still has a Moravian church, though it does not derive directly from Cennick's activities there.

The Moravian church in Bath, organised in 1765 from the Society brought together by Cennick some twenty years earlier, eventually occupied a classical-style building with a Corinthian portico in Charlotte Street, erected in 1845, and later a second one in Coronation Avenue, South Twerton (1907) known as the Cennick Memorial Church. More recently, it has become associated with the Anglican Church of the Ascension in Claude Avenue nearby. Also in Bath is the Weston Free Church (Moravian) which was built in 1953 partly with war-damage compensation on the Fetter Lane Chapel in London, destroyed in an air-raid in May 1941. Inside the church may be seen an historical display featuring a brick from the ruins of the old building dating from 1748 with which, congregationally speaking, Cennick was so much associated and which, according to Hutton, his mother is also said to have attended. In 1992, a plaque was unveiled at 32 Fetter Lane, EC1, to mark the site, between Fleet Street and Holborn Circus.

The Moravian work from Fetter Lane is now located in Chelsea, SW10, where it has maintained a burial ground and small chapel since 1750. Here John Cennick's remains were laid to rest in 1755 and his burial stone can still be seen among those of many other Moravian worthies. The property, which had originally formed part of Sir Thomas More's home in Henry VIII's reign, has been developed as the Moravian Church Exhibition and Visitor Centre, just off King's Road; it contains memorabilia of Cennick's time and regular services are held in the chapel.

During an extended furlough from service in Ireland in 1752, Cennick conducted a wide-ranging tour through much of England, during which he visited and preached at the Moravian settlements at Ockbrook, near Derby, and Fulneck (between Leeds and Bradford). Both of these, with their Georgian chapels, almost certainly used by Cennick, are still in full operation, as is the Gomersal chapel dating from 1751 which was also included in this itinerary. The burial ground at Ockbrook contains the grave of John Cennick's daughter Ann, who died in 1767 at the age of 16.

During this and previous visits to the mainland, Cennick had gone to the Herefordshire town of Leominster, where from around 1740 a small society had been meeting, loosely associated with George Whitefield. Cennick's first visit in 1749 was made at their invitation and led to the establishment of the present Moravian church there in 1759. The foundation stone of the present chapel in South Street was laid the following year. Although, therefore, Cennick did not live to preach in it, his name is still kept in great honour there and a new housing development built on adjacent land by the Marches Housing Association in conjunction with the church was named Cennick Court in memory of him. It was completed in September 2003. Descendants of John Cennick are known to have lived in the vicinity of Thornbury in South Gloucestershire in very recent times.

Finally, mention must be made of traces of Cennick's work still to be seen in Northern Ireland. A H Mumford, in a book published in 1911, stated:

> At Gloonan you can still see Cennick's well, and at Kilwarlin Cennick's tree, and at Portmore (by Lough Beg) Jeremy Taylor's church, where Cennick slept many a night. At Drumargan you can find a barn that was once a Moravian chapel, and a small farmhouse that was once a sisters' house.[4]

These details, however, need to be viewed with some caution. A contemporary Moravian authority in the Province informed the present writer, 'I have never heard of Cennick's tree at Kilwarlin'[5], and the old ruined church of St Lau at Portmore, sometimes indicated as the one Cennick used, was demolished by Cromwell's soldiers whereas Bishop Taylor was not appointed to Ireland until 1661. He did build a new one, known as 'the Middle Church', between Lower and Upper Ballinderry nearby. This still exists and is occasionally used for services but it is not thought to have any link with Cennick's ministry. The barn at Drumargan, if it still exists, may well be the chapel opened by Cennick in 1751.

What can be said with absolute certainty, however, is that three of the five Moravian churches in Northern Ireland today stem directly from John Cennick's ministry. The original chapel at Ballinderry, which he actually helped to build, was opened on Christmas Day 1751, but sadly destroyed by fire and was replaced on the same site by the present one in 1836. Likewise, Kilwarlin, originally dating from 1754, was rebuilt, again where its predecessor had stood, in 1835 after a very successful ministry by a Greek pastor who came when its congregation had dropped to just five people. The third, Gracehill, located at Ballykennedy between Ballymena and Ahoghill, is actually a full-scale Moravian settlement on the original Herrnhut model, incorporating a school, houses for members and other facilities besides the chapel, thus making it the senior one in the Irish District of the denomination. Begun in 1759, it absorbed an earlier congregation at nearby Gloonen, whose chapel was opened by Cennick in 1750, thus giving it a direct link with him. With its graceful Georgian architecture, Gracehill has been designated a conservation area, the first in Northern Ireland. A brand-new facility there opened in June, 2006, is aptly named Cennick Hall.

People from all three congregations were among many who migrated from the country areas to the expanding industrial city of Belfast in the mid to late 19th Century, and after organising themselves through societies and meetings in private dwellings, eventually formed the nucleus of two new Moravian causes in the city, namely University Road and Cliftonville, which are both thriving today and so provide a further, if indirect, link with Cennick's remarkable work in Ireland.

Cennick's Spiritual Legacy

What did John Cennick stand for in his time which endures into the 21st Century? This part of the chapter makes a brief attempt to answer this question. What can be learned afresh from a man who lived in a different age and in a significantly different society?

On his visit to Herrnhaag in 1746, Count Zinzendorf referred to Cennick as 'Paul revived'. In using such an epithet, the Moravian leader claimed that many of the features which adorned the life and work of Paul were also to be found in John Cennick.[6] Although some would argue for the cessation of the title 'Apostle' at the end of the first Christian century, Cennick attracted the informal title 'The Apostle of Wiltshire'. He would not have claimed such a designation for himself, but his life and ministry in the cause of the gospel surely had some Apostolic dimensions, in that he followed Paul in the work of a travelling preacher, establishing communities of Christians wherever he went. As the Apostle to the Gentiles, Paul carried the message of redeeming grace in Christ through most parts of the vast Roman Empire in say 35-65AD. So Cennick, in similar fashion, travelled throughout England, Wales and Ireland between 1740-1755 with essentially the same message and much the same methods.

Paul heralded his confidence in the message he proclaimed in his famous words, 'I am not ashamed of the gospel, because it is the power of God for the salvation of everyone who believes...' (Romans 1:16). It is not difficult to find echoes of this same confidence in the testimony of John Cennick. In his *Personal Creed* he could affirm,

> I believe this Jesus is my God, my Lord, my righteousness, my holiness, my redemption, the only wisdom that can do me good, my Saviour in time and eternity, and I will hereon venture my body and soul for ever and ever.[7]

What he steadfastly believed he would also preach.

The Apostle Paul was not only an evangelist but he was also an apologist. He was concerned that the communities he established should not be drawn away from the purity of the gospel which they had embraced as a result of his preaching. He defended the truth of the message he proclaimed against those who attempted to distort or dilute the gospel and to deny that Christ had the power to transform the lives of those who turned to him in faith. In particular he was concerned that the doctrine of justification by faith in Christ alone should not be adulterated by false ideas about self-reconciliation attained by attending to the requirements of the law. So he could write to the Christians in Galatia, 'Evidently some people are... trying to pervert the gospel of Christ' (Galatians 1:7). In one typical insight into his mind he writes, '...I have you in my heart... defending and confirming the gospel...' (Philippians 1:7).

Although John Cennick was a man of gracious and generous disposition he would not countenance any distortion of the gospel and was an able if reluctant apologist for the orthodox doctrines of salvation which he had found in Scripture and which he had enthusiastically embraced. His *Journal* for 27 February 1751 records a debate with 60 people in Moira (Co. Down, Northern Ireland) concerning the orthodox understanding of the three persons of the Trinity. He comments, 'I know disputes seldom, if ever, have a good effect, yet I thank the Saviour that this did no harm'[8]

Paul had such a confident faith in Christ that his future destiny of heaven was assured by the confirming work of the Holy Spirit. In a well-known biographical testimony toward the end of his eventful life, he could affirm, 'Yet I am not ashamed, because I know in whom I have believed, and am convinced that he is able to guard what I have entrusted to him for that day' (2 Timothy 1:12). If there is one dominant note in Cennick's writings, especially in his hymns, it is that of joyful assurance of sins forgiven, peace with God and the hope of heaven. Typically he can write and sing:

> *Heaven's gate is open to me;*
> *No more hell*
> *Shall prevail,*
> *None can spoil my glory.*[9]

It is these three elements in the ministry of Paul as they are found in the life and work of John Cennick which shape the contours of Cennick's spiritual legacy and which are vital for today's Christian witness to the unchanging Gospel. Cennick exercised an apostolic-style ministry of authoritative evangelism, winning the hearts and minds of thousands of his hearers for Christ and establishing new Christian congregations to the glory of God. Whenever it was required, Cennick would also exercise the ministry of the apologist, stoutly defending the biblical doctrines essential to the purity of the gospel. Cennick's message, as with Paul, never wavered from the centrality of Christ, his redeeming work in the historic and objective events of the incarnation, the sacrificial atonement of the Lamb on the cross, and the subjective reality of experience worked inwardly by the Holy Spirit. Both the objective and the subjective are to be found in this sermon extract:

> Christ died and suffered in our stead. He has borne our curse, he has endured our shame...and he stood like a sinner, and was numbered with the transgressors before God...so we stand perfect and complete in him, being clothed in his righteousness, which is imputed to us, though we did not deserve it...[10]

Some features of Christianity in today's Britain are not dissimilar to those in Cennick's time, others differ greatly. The Christian religion is largely institutionalised as it was in the 18th Century. Many people who are identified with the Christian constituency in Britain may affirm an allegiance to a denominational organisation but bear no clear testimony to Jesus Christ as a personal Saviour. For Cennick, the person and work of Christ was central to his life and his message. He was more concerned with a personal experience of Jesus Christ than with the formal organisation of churches and institutions, despite his episcopalian leanings. He sat quite loosely to ecclesiastical structures and this was true of his beloved Moravian Brethren.

Postmodern Britain is captivated with the concept of celebrity, cultivated by the printed, audio and visual media. Taken to the limits, the 'celebrity' is often an 'idol' and the danger of idolatry is acute and ever present. Young people, in particular, seem to be prone to this insidious hazard. It fills the mind with distractions, a mind which is intended to be filled and captivated by Christ. Some so-called 'celebrities' who affirm a Christian 'faith' maintain that their form of

Christianity is private to them and not a matter for public discussion, despite the clarity of Scripture about the call for all Christians to be a witness to Jesus Christ. John Cennick is a model witness to the work which Jesus Christ had accomplished in his life and he was fearless and tireless in his testimony to the Gospel. He is an excellent example of the dictum, 'We proclaim to you what we have seen and heard' (1 John 1:3).

Postmodern Britain is afraid of absolutes, it is overwhelmed with the notion of tolerance and has all but abandoned any concept of absolute truth; all 'truth' is relative. Thus there is no need to distinguish between various 'faith groups' in the sense that one is superior to another. Postmodern pluralism may have retained its faith in a god of some kind, but if Christianity is to remain true to its origins it will retain its conviction that Jesus Christ is the unique and only full revelation of the eternal God. 'Ye believe in God, believe also in me'– words of Jesus himself which have timeless and absolute relevance. Visser t'Hooft, a former General Secretary of the World Council of Churches, said, 'It is high time Christians rediscovered that Jesus Christ did not come to make a contribution to the religious storehouse of mankind, but that in him, God reconciled the world to himself'.[11] That is the Gospel which Paul in his time and Cennick in his day declared with sharp clarity. It may now be unfashionable but it is still vital and relevant.

Postmodern Britain is afraid of the meta-narrative, the big over-arching story under which all other stories are to be understood. Michael Green writes, 'There is no big story of the world for us to believe, so we are told only a mosaic of little [unconnected] stories... In the absence of an acceptable framework, we must all make our choices...'[12] What suits us, we believe; what we dislike, we discard. It is simply a matter of personal preference rather than 'what is true'. For Cennick, the meta-narrative is that God in his Son has loved the world, and himself has provided the means of reconciling an estranged world to himself. Here is Cennick's *précis* of the meta-narrative, 'When he (Jesus) appeared in the world, it was...as one who undertook to set the whole ruined world to rights...and save his people with justice and equity, and carry away whatever evil came in by the first man'.[13] As Charles Moore wrote recently, 'We are in the bleak mid-winter' of religious confusion.[14] A cloudy mysticism of new-age pseudo-religion has become popular for many people. We could do with the sunshine and warmth of clear scriptural truth to dispel the gloomy intellectualism which pervades much Christian thinking in today's church scene. Cennick stands as a reminder of what God can do through a servant who is dedicated as a vibrant witness to Christ without fear or favour.

Postmodern Britain has little interest in the high standards of morality required by the gospel of Jesus Christ. Many leaders in political, educational, commercial and community service hold loosely to the biblical standards of morality enshrined in the doctrines of sanctification and holiness. Even some seemingly sincere church leaders speak in increasingly muted tones on issues of personal morality and accountability. What I want, I will have, 'because I'm worth it' sums up a mind set which is becoming uncomfortably common. This state of affairs is so pervasive that illustrations abound. It would be tiresome to repeat them. It is to Cennick's credit that there is no discernable stain to be found on his character. This is not to say that he was faultless, but it is difficult to find in him any serious blameworthy conduct.

John Cennick may have drawn away from the doctrine of entire sanctification as understood by John Wesley, at least in his public utterances, but no 18th Century leader exemplified the doctrine of holiness more beautifully than Cennick. Matthew Wilks, one of Whitefield's successors at the Tabernacle in London wrote of Cennick, 'If unaffected humility, deadness to the world, a life of communion with God and a cheerful reliance on a crucified Saviour constitute the real Christian, he was one in eminent degree.'[15] Arnold Dallimore, in his biography of George Whitefield writes:

> So passed from this life at the age of thirty six, the now forgotten John Cennick. He was not only one of the greatest preachers of the 18th Century Revival but also one of its greatest saints. In him Moravianism is seen at its loveliest and best...John Cennick loved the Lord and served him with gladness. For his sake he calmly endured suffering and bore reproach. Jesus, the Lamb of God, filled all his thoughts and captivated all his affections...We are

refreshed by the memory of that simple, inoffensive and mighty man of God, dear, good, and gracious John Cennick.[16]

In the last year of Cennick's life (1755) he wrote to his friend Johannes de Watteville:

I think I have finished with the North of Ireland. I am leaving just at the right time. I am ready to go wherever the Saviour wants me, but best of all would be to go to the Lord himself. If I stay much longer, I fear I shall damage his work![17]

In a personal notebook he wrote:

Now Lord, at peace with Thee and all below,
Let me depart and to Thy Kingdom go:
I long to kiss that hand which once me blessed,
Those feet that travelled to procure my rest;
Those lips that me confessed, and that dear head
That bowed when on it all my sins were laid.[18]

So ended the remarkable life of John Cennick, servant of Christ, evangelist *extraordinaire*, preacher of the Gospel to the lost, prolific hymn-writer, a man of gracious disposition, displaying a constant confidence in God, and who depended for life and eternity on the 'Lamb that was slain'. His first poetic verse was entitled, 'Thus far hath God helped me' and the last words of his own *Nunc dimittis,* 'Stay with the Lamb, and go from Him no more.'

As it was with Abel, so it is with Cennick, 'By faith he was commended as a righteous man...And by faith he still speaks, even though he is dead' (Hebrews 11:4).

References for Chapter 8

[1] N Curnock, ed. *JWJ*, Vol. II, p.175 (footnote)

[2] *ibid.* p.175 (footnote)

[3] J Cennick, *Village Discourses*, p.xv

[4] A H Mumford, *Our Church's Story*, Whightman and Co. Ltd. (London, 1911), p.256

[5] J Cooper, *letter to P Gentry* (2001)

[6] J E Hutton, *John Cennick: A Sketch*, Moravian Publishing Office (London, 1909), p.65

[7] V W Couillard, *The Theology of John Cennick*, *TMHS*, Vol. xvi, Pt. 3, p.112

[8] J Cooper, *EJJC*, p.146

[9] J R Broome, *LHJC*, p.164

[10] V W Couillard, *op.cit.* p.143

[11] W A Visser't Hooft, Former General Secretary of the World Council of Churches, cited M Green, *Adventures of Faith*, Zondervan (Grand Rapids, 2001), p.162

[12] M Green, *Adventures of Faith*, p.155

[13] V W Couillard, *op.cit.* p.142

[14] *The Daily Telegraph*, 10.12.05

[15] A Dallimore, *George Whitefield*, Vol. 2, p.380

[16] *ibid.* p.380

[17] J R Broome, *op.cit.* pp.xiv-xv

[18] *ibid.* p.xv cit., p.xiv

Appendix 1

John Cennick: Chronological Profile

1718
Born in Reading; baptised at St Lawrence Church

1731
Visit to London to find work

1735
'The hand of the Lord touched me'

1737
Conversion at St Lawrence Church, Reading

1739
Visited Oxford to find Charles Kinchin; meeting in Reading with John Wesley; joined Fetter Lane Society, London; preached first sermon at Kingswood, Bristol; appointed to Kingswood School

1740
Began itinerant evangelism in Wiltshire; Wesleys and others left Fetter Lane

1741
Cennick separated from the Wesleys; assisted George Whitefield at Moorfields, London; first collection of hymns published

1742
Whitefield has 'unity' talks with Moravians; Cennick first visited Tetherton (East Tytherton) and purchased property; itinerant evangelism in Wiltshire continues

1744
Tetherton Chapel built; Whitefield leaves Cennick in charge of his work; Dublin Baptists visit London to hear Cennick

1745

Cennick first attempts to visit Dublin; separates from Whitefield to join Moravians

1746

Cennick visits Moravians in Germany; formally linked with Moravians; first visit to Dublin; first visit to north of Ireland (Ballymena); Cennick's Wiltshire societies handed over to Moravians

1747

Cennick's second visit to Germany; lease taken on Skinner's Alley property (Dublin); society formed in Dublin; Cennick married to Jane Bryant; returned to Dublin

1748

Big Butter Lane premises (Dublin) taken by Cennick; Moravian congregation established at Tetherton; Joseph Deane visits Dublin from Ballymena; Cennick's second visit to the north of Ireland; Cennick and family move into house in Crebilly

1749

Cennick has six month visit to London; ordained Deacon in the Moravian Church

1750

Consecration of Chapel at Ballymena; first preached in Belfast

1751

Chapel at Glenavy (Glenevy) dedicated; Lisnamara chapel consecrated (forerunner of Gracehill); chapel at Ballinderry opened

1752

Cennick visits to Moravians at Ockbrook (Derbyshire); visits various places in Yorkshire; visit to Co. Wexford; first General Meeting of Societies in Ballinderry

1753

Itinerant evangelism, chiefly in Wales

1754
Short visit to Dublin to take lease of Big Butter Lane property; preparation for chapel at Kilwarlin; chapel opened at Crosshills; foundation stone laid for Dublin chapel

1755
Ballinderry congregation formally recognised; Dublin chapel opened; Cennick leaves Dublin for London to visit sick mother; Cennick dies in London (age 36); buried in Moravian burial ground in Chelsea

Appendix 2

Cennick's *Personal Creed*

1 I believe that Jesus Christ, who was born in Bethlehem of the Virgin Mary, who suffered under Pontius Pilate without the gates of Jerusalem, is verily, truly and eternally God, the same person all the scriptures mention and speak of, and whom all true believers in all ages have known and worshipped.

2 I believe that God, the whole Godhead by Him, made heaven and earth, and all the worlds, things visible and invisible; that He made me, body and soul, and saw me from His throne in my sinful state, and loved and pitied me, and in due time was a man for my sake; and by His obedience and meritorious life and death has now fully atoned for all my misdeeds and sins, and made me thereby just in the sight of God, and the whole blessed Trinity.

3 I believe this Jesus Christ is my God, my Lord, my righteousness, my holiness, my redemption, the only wisdom which can do me good, my Saviour in time and in eternity, and I will hereon venture my body and soul for ever and ever.

4 I believe also and confess, that though I have been unworthy of His mercy, and no more deserved His favour, yet, out of His free grace, His Holy Spirit has awakened and called me out of my sins, and made me to be concerned about my eternal state, and athirst for mercy and righteousness; that then it pleased the Son of God, my Saviour, to reveal His love in my heart, and to manifest Himself to me, so that now I know I am His and He is mine. He loves me, and I Him; and whether I live or die I am His, who has both lived and died, and rose and revived, that He might be the Lord both of the dead and of the living.

5 I believe when I depart out of this world, I shall go to Him in peace, and when my pilgrimage and warfare is ended, I shall find a rest with Him upon His throne; and, without tasting death, His

angels shall carry me to His bosom, and I shall enter by the gates into the Paradise of God and follow Him upon Mount Zion with the church of the first-born, and with the spirits of just men made perfect, with whom I shall sit down in white raiment in the temple of God and go no more out.

6 I believe that a day shall come when all people shall see the same Jesus that was crucified coming in the clouds; and then every tongue shall confess His divinity and every knee shall bow before Him, who then shall appear in His Father's glory, with all His saints and angels, and shall Himself judge the world in righteousness, and save whom He will. In that day it shall be out of doubt who the Son of Man is, for heaven and earth shall know He is the only Potentate, the God of gods, and Lord of lords, and all those that would not have Him to reign over them shall flee before Him. Then I believe He will confess me and not be ashamed of me, and on this I depend with all my heart. To Him, with His Father, and my Father, and to the Holy Ghost, one God, blessed for ever, be salvation and praise, henceforth world without end.

This *Personal Creed* has been taken from J Cennick, *Village Discourses,* pp.131-132 (Sermon on *The Divinity of Christ*; Matthew 16:13-15; preached in Dublin, 1746) and may be found also in J E Hutton, *John Cennick, A Sketch,* pp.75-76 and V W Couillard, *The Theology of John Cennick,* pp.112-113.

Appendix 3

Cennick's Published Sermons

[Adapted from Couillard's Appendix C and given C identification numbers]

No.	Date	Place Preached	Text	Title
C1*	1739	Kingswood	Mark 15:37	The Cries of the Son of God
C2	1740	Little Somerford (Wiltshire)	Acts 2:38-39	The Gift and Office of the Holy Ghost
C3*	1741	Malmesbury	John 3:3	The New Birth
C4	1742	Bristol	2 Cor. 13:5	The Danger of Infidelity or The Necessity of a Living Faith in Christ
C5*	1743	Bristol	2 Kings 5:13	Naaman Cleansed
C6*	1743	London	Mark 5:34	The Bloody Issue Healed
C7*	1744	Plymouth	Acts 22:16	St Paul's Conversion
C8	1744	St Genys (Cornwall)	John 10:14	The Good Shepherd
C9	1744	Bidford	Matthew 7:24	The Best Foundation
C10	1744	London	Luke 10:37	The Good Samaritan
C11	1744	Exeter	Luke 7:48	Simon and Mary
C12	1744	Exeter	Genesis 24:31	The Marriage of Isaac
C13	1745	London	Hebrews 8:7	The Two Covenants
C14	1745	London	Hebrews 12:22-24	The Benefits of the New Testament
C15*	1746	Dublin	Matthew 16:13-15	The Divinity of Christ
C16	1748	Co. Antrim	Mark 4:9	The Sower

C17*	1750	Co. Antrim	Luke 15:2	The Lost Sheep, Piece of Silver and Prodigal Son
C18	1750	London	Matthew 15:28	The Syrophoenician: or a Pattern of Invincible Faith
C19	1751	North of Ireland	Colossians 2:17	The Shadows of Christ
C20	1752	Ballynahone (Co. Tyrone)	1 Cor. 15:47	The Fall and Redemption
C21*	1752	Scholes (Yorks)	John 4:10	The Woman of Samaria
C22	1752	North of Ireland	Hebrews 5:12	The First Principles of Christianity
C23	1752	North of Ireland	Isaiah 53:11	The Sufferings and Satisfaction of Christ
C24	1753	Dublin	Matthew 5:3	The Beatitudes
C25	1753	Haverfordwest	Luke 8:39	The Demoniac
C26	1753	Dublin	Luke 16:31	Dives and Lazarus
C27	1753	Milford Haven	Matthew 13:44	The Hidden Treasure
C28	1753	Haverfordwest	Luke 4:18-19	The Offices of the Messiah
C29*	1753	Bath	Hebrews 9:26	The Great Sacrifice
C30	1753	Pembroke	Genesis 19:17	Lot's Flight
C31	1753	Kingswood	John 8:21	Deliverance from Death
C32	1754	Grogan (Co. Antrim)	John 1:12	The Privilege of Believers
C33	1754	Ballinderry (Co. Antrim)	1 Tim. 1:15-16	The Patterns of Mercy
C34	1754	Dublin	Ezekiel 37:14	The Vision of Dry Bones

C35	1754	London	Ezekiel 9:6	The Safety of a True Christian
C36*	1754	Glenavy (Co. Antrim)	Isaiah 38:17	The Assurance of Faith: or The Experience of a True Christian
C37	1754	Drumargan (Co. Antrim)	Deut. 22:11	The Linsey-Woolsey Garment
C38	1754	Gloonan (Co. Antrim)	Hebrews 13:3	The Reproach of the Cross
C39	1755	Unknown	Luke 7:13	The Widow of Nain
C40*	1755	Ballymena (Co. Antrim)	John 1:29	The Beautiful Vision: or Beholding Jesus Crucified

For further details of Cennick's corpus of sermons see F Baker, *PWHS,* Vol. xxx, 1955, Pts. 3-4.

Appendix 4

Moravians and the Bible

In his two-volume biography of George Whitefield, Arnold Dallimore makes the following rather surprising assertion:

> 'Moravianism differed from all other sections of the Revival in that it did not fully accept the Scriptures as the Word of God. Count Zinzendorf held that the Bible contained both truth and error. Therefore, it was not regarded among the Moravian people as the sole source of spiritual authority...'[1]

Dallimore uncharacteristically gives no source or authority for his claim, but coming from such a respected historian, it deserves notice and some investigation.

Clifford W Towlson in his study *Moravian and Methodist* refers to a tract dating from about 1755 entitled *Queries humbly proposed to the right reverend and right honourable Count Zinzendorf* which dealt with, among other subjects, 'the Moravians' alleged contempt for the Bible...' No source or reference is given.[2] Later in the same work Towlson quotes a letter from Charles Wesley to John Fletcher, dated 22 February 1772, in which he remarked of the Moravians, 'they did sadly halt and strongly incline to Antinomianism and drew us into their error...their famous Count fairly turns St James out of the Canon.'[3]

In his study of the Oxford Methodists, Luke Tyerman observed, 'Moravianism, always eccentric, was now becoming arrogant' and quoted John Gambold, an Oxford Methodist who became a Moravian Bishop, as saying in a letter vindicating the Count, 'he also likes very much to translate the scriptures in a free, round manner, and in modern words.'[4]

The present writers are of the view that any irregularity on Biblical soundness was limited to Zinzendorf's negative view of the Epistle of James with its stress on works as evidence of faith, which would naturally follow from his Lutheran upbringing and background. Luther himself had branded James 'an epistle of straw and destitute of evangelic character.' In thus expressing the same view, perhaps injudiciously, the Count may have given some Moravians the idea that the Bible generally was not entirely to be believed as the truth, and in the volatile and unstable atmosphere of the Brethren's 'Sifting Time', the issue may have been blown up out of proportion. It doubtless passed into oblivion along with 'stillness' and other excesses of the period.

Dallimore's rather sweeping assertion is wide of the mark and applies to the whole Moravian movement an aberration confined to Zinzendorf's personal views and which has not shaped the Moravian Church's theology or affected its loyalty to the Bible. Of the latter there is no doubt, as is clear from its officially declared position:

> 'The Triune God as revealed in the Holy Scripture of the Old and New Testaments is the only source of our life and salvation; and this Scripture is the sole standard of the doctrine of faith of the Unitas Fratrum and therefore shapes our life.'[5]

It is clear to the present authors, from all that Cennick wrote and preached that he did not hold to any liberal views on the final authority of Scripture.

---

[1] A Dallimore, *George Whitefield*, Banner of Truth Trust (Edinburgh, 1980), Vol. 2, p.325

[2] C W Towlson, *Moravian and Methodist*, Epworth Press (London, 1957), p.146

[3] *ibid.* p.155

[4] L Tyerman, *The Oxford Methodists*, Hodder and Stoughton (London, 1873), p.190

[5] Church Order of the Unitas Fratrum, 1995, (God's Word and Doctrine p.14)

Bibliography

The following should not be regarded as a complete listing of all the writings associated with the life and work of John Cennick. What follows is a listing of works which the present authors have found helpful, and is given as a guide to the sources on which the book is based and to help with further research. The Bibliography is a supplement to the chapter reference notes.

The Bicentennial edition of Wesley's Works will replace all previous editions but because this remains incomplete the authors have chosen to use the older editions except for the Bicentennial edition of Volume 7.

F Baker, *J Cennick: A Handlist of his Writings*, Proceedings of the Wesley Historical Society, Vol. xxx, Pts. 2-5 (1955)

A D Belden, *George Whitefield: The Awakener* (London, 1930)

V Best, *A History of the Ballinderry Moravian Church* (Antrim, 2000)

W C Braithwaite, *The Beginnings of Quakerism* (London, 1912)

J R Broome, *Life and Hymns of John Cennick, LHJC* (Harpenden, 1988)

D A Carson, *A Call to Spiritual Reformation* (Grand Rapids, Michigan, 1992)

F Cook, *Our Hymn-writers and their Hymns* (Darlington, 2005)

V W Couillard, *The Theology of John Cennick* (*TMHS,* Vol. xvi, Pt. 3, 1957)

J H Cooper, *Extracts from the Journals of John Cennick*: *EJJC* Moravian Evangelist (Antrim, 1996)

N Curnock, ed. *The Journal of John Wesley, JJW*, Standard Edition (London, 1938)

BOLD AS A LION

A A Dallimore, *George Whitefield: The Life and Times of the great Evangelist of the 18th Century Revival*, 2 Vols. (London, 1970; Edinburgh, 1980)

A L Fries, *Customs and Practices of the Moravian Church*, Moravian Board of Education and Evangelism (1973)

J H Foy, *Moravians in Ireland* (1986)

P Gubi, *Whither John Cennick?*, Unpublished MA Dissertation (Bristol, 1998)

E Houghton, *Christian Hymn-Writers* (Bridgend, Glamorgan, 1988)

Edward Houghton, *The Handmaid of Piety*, The Wesley Fellowship, Lutterworth, 1992)

J E Hutton, *John Cennick - A Sketch* (London, undated)

J E Hutton, *The History of the Moravian Church* (London, 1909)

A G Ives, *Kingswood School in Wesley's Day and Since* (Epworth, 1957)

T Jackson, *The Life of The Rev Charles Wesley*, MA (London, 1841)

H A L Jefferson, *Hymns in Christian Worship* (London, 1950)

W Leary, *John Cennick: A Bi-centenary Appreciation*, *PWHS*, Vol. xxx, Pt. 2 (1955)

J Leighton, *Howell Harris: The 18th Century Exhorter* (London, 1972)

B L Manning, *The Hymns of Wesley and Watts* (London, 1948)

H B McGonigle, *Sufficient Saving Grace: John Wesley's Evangelical Arminianism* (Carlisle, 2001)

H B McGonigle, *John Wesley and the Moravians* (Lutterworth, 1993)

A H Mumford, *Our Church's Story* (London, 1911)

J L Nuelson, *John Wesley and the German Hymn* (Calverly, Yorkshire, 1972)

C Podmore, *The Moravian Church in England 1728-1760* (Oxford, 1998)

C Podmore, ed. *The Fetter Lane Moravian Congregation* 1742-1992 (London, 1992)

J Pollock, *John Wesley* (London, 1989)

H Rack, *Reasonable Enthusiast: John Wesley and the Rise of Methodism* (London, 1992)

M Schmidt, *John Wesley: A Theological Biography, 2 Vols.* (London, 1962, 1971)

A C H Seymour, *The Life and Times of Selina, Countess of Huntingdon* (London, 1844)

G and M Stead, *The Exotic Plant: A History of the Moravian Church in Britain 1742-2000* (Peterborough, 2003)

R Strong, *The Moravians at Fulneck* (Fulneck, 1993)

J Telford, *The Methodist Hymn-Book Illustrated in History and Experience* (London, 1959)

J Telford, ed. *The Letters of John Wesley, Standard Edition LJW* (London, 1931)

C W Towlson, *Moravian and Methodist: Relationships and Influences in the Eighteenth Century* (London, 1957)

L Tyerman, *The Oxford Methodists* (London, 1873)

C E Vuilliamy, *John Wesley* (London, 1933)

J R Watson, *The English Hymn: A Critical and Historical Study* (Oxford, 1999)

G Watson, *Celestial Anthems*: *Poems by John Cennick CA* (Reading, 2001)

R White, *A History of Gracehill Moravian Settlement* (Antrim, 1996)

A Skevington Wood, *The Inextinguishable Blaze: Spiritual Renewal and Advance in the Eighteenth Century* (London, 1960)

A Skevington Wood, *Luther's Principles of Biblical Interpretation* (London, 1960)

JOHN CENNICK

INDEX OF PERSONS AND PLACES

Adair, Captain Robert	58
Ahoghill	144
Aldersgate Street	123
America	7,20,21,25,26,27,38,41,45,51,53,122,123
Anna of Bohemia, Princess	49
Antrim, Co.	58,60,68,90,104,110,129,157-59, 162,165
Armagh, Co	60,167
Arrat, (Mr)	76,77
Athanasius	79
Ayling/Allen, Ann	32
Ballee	96
Ballinderry	4,60-62,68,144,153,154,158,162
Ballykennedy	144
Ballymena	58-60,95,144,154,161
Bath	8,26,28,39,53,61,62,141,142,158
Bedford	62,65
Belden, A D	44,48,53,66,162
Berridge, J	18
Bethlehem Chapel	49
Biddle, John	78
Big Butter Lane	153,154
Brace,D	8
Builth Wells	96
Bohemia	14,15,49,50,52
Böhler, Peter	51,54,55,83,103
Bowood House	78
Bradford-on-Avon	39
Braithwaite	13,23,162
Bridgeyate	30
Brinkworth	39,40
Bristol	3,4,8,22,24,25,26,27,28,29,30,32,33,43,45, 53,64,68, 73,82,83,89,90,100,101,132,137, 140,152,157,163
Bryant, (Bro)	39,40
Bryant, Jane	63,153

Caerphilly	44
Cambridge	94
Carey, William	51
Carlisle, Thomas	117
Castle Combe	38,68,141
Cavan, Co.	60
Cell, George Croft	75
Cennick, Ann	9,64,68,143
Cennick, Anna	14,15,64
Cennick, Anna (Mrs)	19,22,42,64
Cennick Hannah Elizabeth (later Swertner)	64

Cennick, John
Christology	18,58,78-82,87,100,145,147
Disputes	30-34,38,46,53,55,58,60,81,141
Family	14,15,19,63,64,65,72,140
Hymns	56,113-133
Preaching	29,30,38,40,44,46,55,57,60,61,63,76,82, 95-108,147,
Personal Creed	74,79,80,81,107,108,145,155,156
Sermons	26,58,63,73,81,82,83,93,100-108,130,157,159
Theology	22,31,32,33,52,54,55, 56,58,71-75, 78-88,100,102,104,105,107,147,149

Cennick, Sally	15,21,22
Charles I	13
Charles II	14,61
Charleston	122
Cheapside	16
Chelsea	63,68,142,154
Chester	56
Chippenham	30,39,142
Clack (Bradenstoke)	63
Cliftonville (Belfast)	144
Coke, T	28,35
Connor, Margaret	8
Cullodon	58
Cooper, Bishop J H	8,10,35,48,66,67,81,89,90,109,151,162
Cootehill	60

Corsham	39
Couillard, V W	76,80,81,84,85,87,89,90,91,101,106,107, 109,110,111,151,156,157,162,165
Crebilly	60,96,153
Cromwell	144
Crosshills	60,154
Cudworth, William	46
Curtis, T&A	14
Daily Watchwords	63
Dallimore, Arnold	55,63,66,67,94,109,137,149,151,160,161,163
Dauntsey	39
David, Christian	50,51
Davis, Ann	32
Davis, Margaret	96
de Watteville, Johannes	150
Deal (Kent)	20
Deane, Joseph	58,59,95,153
Derry, Co.	60
Derryscollop	60
Doagh	60
Dober, Leonard	55
Donegal, Co	60
Down, Co	77,146
Dublin	4,55-61,63,68,73,74,95,101,152,156,157,158
Dummer	20,21
Edwards, Samuel	59
Elizabeth, Princess (later Elizabeth II)	65
Elverton	30
Emerson	123
Epworth	10,36,48,66,72,89,132,134,136,161,163
Exeter	10,32,45,157
Ferne, (Bro.)	29
Fetter Lane	21,31,51,52,56,63,64,68,94,103,142,152,164
Foundery, The	29,31,41,56
Fox, George	13
Fulneck (Bradford)	8,51,63,65,68,129,143,164
Gambold,J	160
Geneva	78

Georgia (USA)	26,41,52,54,122,123
Gerhardt, Paul	117,118,119,120,135
German(y)	31,34,49,50,54,57,59,62,64,65,73,82,116,117 118,122,123,134,153,164
Glenavy	60,153,159
Gloonan	60,143,159
Gloucester(shire)	26,30,38,43,45,73,143
Gomersal	65,143
Gotly, (Bro.)	39,40
Gracehill	4,62,63,68,129,144,153,165
Graham, William T	8,89
Green, Michael	148,151
Greenlee, Dr G	8
Grimshaw, W	18
Grogan	60,158
Gubi, Peter	8,82,90,128,137,142,163
Hambrook	30
Hanham Mount	141
Harris, Howell	6,18,27,43,44,45,46,48,94,163
Harrison, A W	46
Hastings, Elizabeth	61
Haverfordwest	9,62,67,158
Herrnhut	51,54,144
Hervey, J	21,173
Holmes, Wendell	123
Holyhead	57,63
Hullavington	39
Humphreys, J	30,41,44,45
Hungary	50
Huntingdon, Earl of	13
Huntingdon, Selina Countess of	28,35,37,52,61,66,164
Hus, John	50
Hutton, Jonathan	8
Hutton, J E	8,13,20,23,24,28,29,31,32.35,36,37,45,48, 52,55,62,64,66,67,82,83,90,109,142,151,161, 163
Hutton, James	21
Ingham, Benjamin	51,62,94
Ireland	4,7,8,22,55-62,65,73,77,79,81,102,111,

Jefferson, H A L	133,143,144,145,146,153,158,163
	118,120,135,136,163
Jerusalem	115,155
Jesus Christ	6,18,21,52,53,61,74,75,78,79,80,81,82,87,98,
	100,101,104,107,115,124,128,129,145,147,
	148,149,155,156,159
Jones, Griffith	44
Keen, Sylvester	97
Kellaways (Tetherton-Callaways)	39
Kendalshire	30
Kethe, William	117
Kilwarlin	60,62,68,143,144,154
Kinchin,C	20,21,153
Kingswood	22,27,28,29,30,31,32,33,34,37,38,41,42,43,
	45,52,53,59,62,64,68,72,83,89,130,140,141,
	152,155,158,163
Kington Langley	39
La Trobe, Benjamin	57,59,60
Lacey,A	9
Langley Burrell	30
Lansdown (Bath)	28,141
Laud (Archbishop)	13
Leary, William	33,36,48,72,89,163
Leominster	62,96,143
Leprosy	76
Lewis, D M	6
Lindheim	54
Lineham,P	6,64,67
Lisnamara	60,153
Little, J	8
Littleton Drew	39
London	7,8,10,11,16,21,22,23,25,26,29,30,31,33,35,
	36,37,41,42,43,45,46,47,48,51,52,54,55,56,
	59,62,63,64,65,66,6,68,73,89,90,109,110,
	132,133,134,135,136,137,142,149,151,152,
	153,154,155,157,158,159,161,162,163,164,
	165,167
Luther (Lutheran)	50,51,62,63,75,77,90,116,117,160
Lutterworth, Leicestershire	49,89,163

Lyneham	39
Malmesbury	39,62,90,142,157
Manning. B L	124,125,136,163
Marienborn	54,73,123
Maxfield, Thomas	29,30
McGonigle,Revd Dr H	5,9,85,89,90,163
Merchant Venturers	25
Moira (Irerland)	61,77,146
Mölther, Philip	31,56
Monaghan, Co	60
Monarchism	78
Montgomery, James	63,129
Moore, Charles	148
Moore, H	28,35,
Moore, T	65
Moorfields	31,41,43,45,47,53,56,153
Moravian(s)	1,3,4,5,6,8,9,10,11,14,21,22,23,30,31,34,35, 45,46,48-69,,71,72,73,74,77, 78,82,83,84, 86,87,88,89,90,96,97,103,109,114,118,122, 123,124,127,128,129,136,141,142,143,144, 145,147,149,151,153,154,155,160,-165
More, Sir Thomas	142
Morton, J	8
Mount Hill	141
Mumford, A H	67,99,100,110,143,151,163
Munsey Turner, John	75,89
Nathen, Sammy	29
Neale, John Mason	114,134
New England (USA)	55
New Kilpatrick	42
Newton, John	18
Nicea	79
Northampton	62
Nottingham	62
Nuelson, J L	122,134,135,136,137,164
Ockbrook (Derby/shire)	9,51,62,64
O'Neil, Lord	61
Orchard, William	38
Oxford	6,11,20,21,23,26,66

Parsons, Lorraine   8
Paul (Apostle)   87,102,107,115,145,146,147,148,159
Peden, Alexander   61
Penn, William   13
Podmore, Colin   83,90,93,103,109,110,164
Poland   50,78
Pollock, J   32,35
Pope, The   57
Portmore   61,95,143,144
Powell   44
Prague (Czechoslovakia)   50
Price, Thomas   44
Priestley, Joseph   78,79
Prussia   50
Pursey, A   9
Rae, M   9
Rawdon, Lord   61
Reading   10,13,14,16,17,21,22,68,69,74,140,152,165
Rhosgoch   96
Richard II   49
Rider, Bishop John   60
Roche, John   55
Ronneburg Castle   54
Rothe, JA   51
Rowde   39,40
Rowlands, Daniel   44
Sabellianism   78
Salisbury   16
Saxony   49,50,54
Seeds, N   9
Schmidt, M   33,36,107
Scholes (Yorks)   104,110,158
Scotland   7,42,129
Seagrave, Robert   41
Seagry   39
Seward, W   28
Seymour, A C H   28,35,52,66,164
Shane's Castle   60,61
Sheffield   129,137

Simeon, C	18
Simmonds	122
Skinner's Alley	57,58,63,68,95,153
Sodbury	38
Somerford	39,157
South Twerton	142
Southampton	121
Sozzini, F	78
Sozzini, L	78
Spangenburg	53
St Augustine of Hippo	114
St Francis Xavier	57
St Lau (Portmore)	144
St Lawrence's Church	14,17,68,74,140,152
St Patrick's Cathedral	95
Stevens, Abel	29,35
Stoke Newington Academy	121
Stratton (St Margaret's)	39,97
Sutton Benger	39
Swaddlers	58
Swertner, John	64,167
Swertner, Louisa	64
Swindon	39,43,97,142
Syston	30
Tabernacle(s)	41,42,43,45,46,47,53,56,68,133,141,149
Taylor, Bishop Jeremy	61,143
Telford, John	10,24,35,48,63,66,67,134,136,164
Temple Bar	21
Tennent, Gilbert	55
Tersteegen, Gerhardt	123,136
t'hooft, Visser	148,151
Thornbury	143
Tippet, Stephen	37
Tockington	30
Toeltschig, Johann	52,59,60
Towlson, Clifford	51,66,72,89,160,161,164,
Trevecca	45
Turton, Bro.	96
Tyerman, L	55,66,98,109,160,164

Tyrone, Co.	60,160
Tytherton (East&West)	8,39,40,45,62,63,64,68,142,152
always rendered as 'Tetherton'	
in Cennick's writings)	
University Road (Belfast)	144
Upton Cheyney (near Bath)	39
Violet, J and T	97
Von Carlstadt, Andreas	116
Vulliamy, C E	73,89
Wales	7,15,44,62,73,102,103,134,145,153
Watkins, Bro.	94
Watson, G	10,13,15,23,24,49,109,129,134,135,136,
	137,165
Watson, J R	114,134,135,164
Watts, Isaac	114,117,120,121,124,125,130,132,136,163
Webb, R	9,67
Weiss, John Paul	54
Wesley, Charles	26,31,32,33,48,83,94,98,109,118,121,124,
	125,127,131,132,136,163,166
Wesley, John	4,7,10,11,14,19,20,21,26,27,28,30,32,34,35,
	36,46,51,52,56,58,59,61,63,64,72,75,86,89,
	94,98,103,107,109,113,118,122,123,124,126,
	134,140,149,152,162,163,164
Wesley, Susanna	30
West Indies	25,51
West Kington	39
Westerleigh	30
Wexford	61,153
Whitefield, G	4,6,7,10,18,19,20,21,22,26,27,28,31,33,34,
	37,38,40,41,42,43,44,45,46,47,48,51,52,53,
	55,61,63,66,68,71,72,73,83,84,86,94,95,100,
	101,104,106,109,110,128,133,137,140,141,
	143,149,151,152,153,160,161,162,163
White's Alley	103
Wilde, Oscar	13
Wilks, Matthew	23,35,47,48,66,110,149
Williams, Thomas	59
Williams, William	44
Wilmot, K	21

Wiltshire	7,30,38,40,43,45,53,56,62,63,64,68,73,83, 95,109,141,142,145,152,153,157
Wood, A S	14,77
Wycliffe	49,50
Yorkshire	7,51,62,62,68,69,78,104,110,113,134, 153,164
Zinzendorf, Count	50,51,54,64,82,86,103,122,124,127,128,129, 145,160,161